Exiles and Communities

SUNY Series, Feminist Theory in Education

Madeleine R. Grumet, Editor

Other books in this series include:

Changing Education: Women as Radicals and Conservators
                    —Joyce Antler and Sari Knopp Biklen (eds.)

Exiles and Communities

Teaching in the Patriarchal Wilderness

Jo Anne Pagano

State University of New York Press

Published by
State University of New York Press, Albany

© 1990 State University of New York

For information, address State University of New York
Press, State University Plaza, Albany, N.Y., 12246

Library of Congress Cataloging-in-Publication Data

Pagano, Jo Anne, 1946–
    Exiles and communities : teaching in the patriarchal wilderness /
Jo Anne Pagano.
        p.   cm. — (SUNY series in feminist theory in education)
    Includes bibliographical references.
    ISBN 0-7914-0273-8. — ISBN 0-7914-0274-6 (pbk.)
    1. Pagano, Jo Anne, 1946– .   2. Women teachers—United States—
Biography.   3. Sex differences in education—United States.   4. Feminist
criticism—United States.   I. Title.   II. Series.
LA2317.P28A3   1990
371.1′0092′2—dc20   89-29352
                                                                            CIP

10   9   8   7   6   5   4   3   2   1

Contents

Foreword

Merleau-Ponty has reminded us that it is in a world already spoken that we speak. He understood that with every utterance we announce ourselves as members of human and historical communities. Our choices and expressions of meaning are connected to what has mattered in this world to the people who have cared for us. Nevertheless, his sense of language is not locked in a ritual incantation of our ancestors' sayings. Merleau-Ponty also understood the flexibility of language. He knew we could make old words do somersaults and that we could fly between them like trapeze artists.

Jo Anne Pagano's meditations on teaching celebrate and perform our power to make new worlds out of old words. It isn't easy work, as we all know. The pull of the old path is powerful. To say it as HE said it, to repeat it as they all did, is to thread a catechism even through language that rings with authority, intellect and style. Comforting, weren't they, those cadences of our parents and teachers, and the homilies they quoted, and the seers they cited.

Acknowledging the lure and lair of the normative, Jo Anne Pagano takes on the beast with, you might say, her bare hands. She does not deploy feminist theory like a whip. She is no terrorist. She does not drill us in the proper dogma and sentiments. She is no martinet. Nor does she hook up her wagons and move her show to the edge of town where she will avoid comparisons with legitimate theatre. Instead, she walks calmly and deliberately into the ring, drums rolling, hoops burning, trumpets blaring, and teaches the beast new tricks.

She shows us what we must do as feminist educators. The show goes on, and we sell the tickets, hawk the cotton candy, wriggle into sequinned satin and dance with the bears. But from Madison Square Garden to Peoria we work to transform the performance and performers. We work to make new meanings out of old words.

This work is at once playful and serious. Pagano raises serious questions irreverently: "How are we implicated in what we know? What actions are required by our knowledge?" She asks us how women who teach are different from our male predecessors and colleagues and from the knowledge we rent from them. She asks us what right we have to tell others our stories and what authority we can summon to justify our intrusions into other people's thoughts and activity. She extends her meditations on these foundational issues in the philosophy of education into literature, psychoanalytic theory and into descriptions of her own work with students. After a while, she has edged these issues so far off their foundations that it looks as if an antic wind has just come down their street, lifted each issue up and set it down again where the light is better.

But Jo Anne Pagano does not desert the old neighborhood even as she relocates and rezones our rights and obligations. As Jo Anne Pagano remembers the words which spoke the world in which she learned to speak and read and write, she offers us both her old and new readings. Often children like to amuse us and themselves by recounting their former misapprehensions of the world. "I used to think that Tisofthee was the name of our country." "I used to think that when a ship went through the locks you could see little red fishes swimming all around it." One is always less than completely convinced that the young narrator is fully converted to the new truth.

Pagano has not forgotten the power of her old ideas. She shows us how to think differently about experience without repudiating it. She still has affection for what she leaves behind. And in that affection she gives us important lessons in feminist pedagogy: respect for the specificity of experience, for the power of desire, for the person you were, the person you are and are not, and for the person you would change.

By holding a conversation with her dearest old books and fervent convictions, Pagano provides more than a dialogue. The space between what she used to think and what she now thinks is inviting and joined by conversations with students, with Ryle and Socrates, with Woolf and Sarton, with Homans and Lacan, with you and me.

I can't speak for Ryle and Woolf or for you, but I can tell you how it has been for me to be included in this conversation. If you write words for a living, there is always the danger they will be only that—your capital, things of yours that accumulate interest whenever they are cited. If you would write living words, someone must take them up and make them into something else. One who receives them so transforms them into a gift, for as in Lewis Hyde's appraisal, a gift is an object that always moves from one person to another, ever augmented by each person's use of it. Transformed by the alchemy of her attention, my words are drawn into the world of this text where they find new life.

Teachers have always talked together about their work, lingering by the mailboxes, brown bagging it in the lounge. Feminist theory in education needs to recapture and extend our conversations into the texts that record what we know and want to know about our work as educators.

The style of this prose is its lesson and moral. Jo Anne Pagano teaches us how to teach as she sustains identity in transformation, and relinquishes neither the world nor other people to thought. The conversations of this text weave together descriptions of practice, questions of ethics, theories of gender, analyses of knowledge, the kitchen stove and the cats. In some texts the last two items would be seen as impostors in this series of pedagogical terms. But, as Jo Anne Pagano would insist, they belong here. And so do we.

Madeleine R. Grumet
May, 1989

Acknowledgments

In the introduction to this book, I wrote, "Even when we talk to ourselves, we're talking to someone else." I acknowledge now the importance to this book of good talk with friends and colleagues. They're everywhere in this book. My students at Colgate University are here, too. There would be no book without them, or without my colleagues on the faculty here. Everything I claim to know about teaching, I learned from my students and my colleagues. I am grateful to the members of the feminist theory study group at Colgate for the monthly conversations. They're here, too. My own teachers are everywhere here, too, especially William Pinar whose own work first got me involved with educational theory. With affection I thank Madeleine Grumet for listening even when she didn't know I was talking to her. I thank her too for the gift of her work and for the conversation that hums beneath this book. Without her encouragement and support, and without the invitation to participate expressed in her own work, this book would not exist. The following people have also been important: Landon Beyer, Peter Taubman, Janet Miller, Jane Pinchin, Jill Harsin, Margaret Maurer, Kay Johnston, Tony Whitson, Walter Feinberg, Ann Lane, Lynn Schwarzer, John Knecht, and Joan Thompson. I am grateful to Colgate University for a semester's leave which permitted me to begin this work. Finally, for listening, for talking, for reading, and for caring, and for understanding the middle distance, I thank my husband, Bruce Berlind. This book is about that.

Introduction

I am a teacher, and I am a woman. I am a woman who teaches. I am a female teacher. I don't mean that I am a teacher because I am a woman. In my case I am a teacher despite my being a woman. This is important to everything that follows. Until I actually began teaching, I disdained the profession because of its press as nice work for a woman, and probably because of its association with women's work. As recently as ten years ago I was unconscious of the way in which my profession and my sex complicated each other. As far back as ten years ago and longer, ever since I began to teach, certain doubts and questions and confusions have kept up a steady and distracting noise beneath the daily conversations which are the teacher's work.

Every teacher of the poor and disenfranchised knows that teaching is through and through political. My high school students in the mid-1970s taught me that. All teaching is political, even teaching which disclaims its politics, even teaching the children of the privileged classes. For to teach is to bring others to look at things in new ways, to reorient them to the horizon of their world. That we are changed in the process of education is no mere accident. We teachers want to change our students. And we are certain that the change is for the better. "Yes, but," some say, "literature, art, history, philosophy, science—these are not political." If this were true, churches and governments would be unlikely to have devoted themselves to suppressing scientific discoveries, literature, and histories as strenuously as various of them at various times have. Copernicus' displacement of the earth from the center of the universe ramified throughout the religious, social, and political worlds. Darwinian natural selection deeply disturbed our notions of humanness, and Freud's discovery of unconscious motivation made it impossible for us to rely even on ourselves. Photography, painting, and architecture have been known to transform our experience of physical space. Whether one thinks of the universe as an organism or a machine, whether one thinks events random or ordered makes all the difference there is. What we believe we know about human nature, about the principles of economics, even what we believe we know about what makes good literature or art has everything to do with how we choose to live our lives. I insist that any knowledge or understanding is political because we come to the world and situate ourselves there through what we know and understand. For this reason, education is both intensely personal and intensely political.

Through education we enter a cultural conversation, always somewhere in the middle. There we find and form our understanding of ourselves and our communities. Some are already fluent in the language in which the conversation takes place. Some are familiar with its referents and with the tricks of politeness which keep the talk flowing. They easily find their places in the world. But some never catch the drift of the conversation. Others are bored. Some hesitate too long and never get a word in. The conversation puts them in their places.

Because I believe what I believe, I am alive to the fact that the practice of teaching is morally charged. To believe that in the present epistemological scene is to let yourself in for big trouble. Contemporary philosophy, social science, and literary theory have accustomed most of us to perceive authority and authorship as these are judged, achieved, or conferred as products of human interest, and to understand that human interest is socially and historically conditioned—that knowledge itself is institutional. We have been comfortable for some time now with texts which have no stable meanings, with the shift of authority from the text to the interpretation of the text; we have learned to inhabit a world in which knowledge claims are judged according to standards of truthfulness rather than of truth; we live with the suspicion that social research constitutes, in an important sense, its phenomena. If this is true, if knowledge is indeed constitutive of the world, then our choices about what to teach, how to teach, and how to interpret the texts we teach are ethical choices. They are choices about the sort of world we want to live in. They are choices about what sort of life that world will support. They are choices about a consciousness that projects the world.

In graduate school, studying the philosophy of education, I encountered any number of philosophers bent on pinning down precisely those things about the act of teaching which made it teaching rather than something else. These philosophers always insisted that for an act to be considered an act of teaching, it had to occur within the context of a triadic relationship, a relationship limited by the formula A teaches X to B—someone teaches something to someone else. We are not surprised when this formulation starts to give us some trouble. What should I call it when I teach myself to play the piano? The next condition regularly adduced is that teaching be intentional. A must intend to teach X to B. There are interesting problems here, too, now that researchers have found the hidden curriculum and discovered unintentional teaching outcomes. Teaching well, teaching poorly, these would have to wait for another time. Still, teaching was relatively simple. When we got to education (when is a teacher educating?), we could no longer avoid the moral question. For teaching to be educating, R. S. Peters and others told us, the outcome ought to be thought to be worthwhile. Education, Peters told us, is a word that functions like the word "reform." If one is indeed educating, one is engaged in worthwhile teaching. And a worthwhile education achieves such ends as an enlarged cognitive capacity, breadth of understanding, etc. Now I really had a hard time with all of that. I kept saying to myself, "Yes, but. . . ."

Knowing the meanings of words did not make me any more certain than I had been before that I was doing a good thing. To tell me that the process of education transmits what is most worthwhile in a culture across the generations gave me small comfort. For how would I know what is most worthwhile? And which culture should I choose from? To know is to make that decision. To know is to know oneself as a knower. To know is to know the world in a made image. To know is to enact that image. I could not have this conversation with the philosophers. We did not speak the same language.

When Dorothy first meets the witch Glinda in the land of Oz, Glinda asks her whether she is a good witch or a bad witch. Dorothy stammers, "Who, me? Why I'm not a witch at all. I'm Dorothy Gale from Kansas." Glinda then points to Toto and says, "Well then is that the witch?" Dorothy's negative response leaves Glinda totally at a loss. As she says, "There's your house, and there's the witch of the east—dead, and so what the Munchkins want to know is, are you a good witch or a bad witch?" Given certain assumptions, the question follows. But, of course, as Dorothy already knew, Oz isn't a bit like Kansas. I sometimes felt like Dorothy in the Land of Oz. I just wanted to go home to Kansas where people weren't always coming and going in such peculiar ways.

Now, of course, I understood that frame of reference was everything. Only in Kansas are all witches old and ugly. In Oz things are different. There were philosophers and theorists of literature and social science to assure me that actions and claims could be adjudicated by reference to a community of knowers. I shouldn't worry anymore about objectivity or certainty in the old sense. I would know that everything was all right if we all agreed. The intersubjective judgments of the community were the final appeal. The heat was off me. "Yes, but. . . ." Like any dogged undergraduate I wanted to know, "Was this a good community or a bad one?" Did it matter after all since there was no place else to be but in it? One has no choice about these matters. We call people who choose otherwise crazy. Still, I was not present at the signing of the agreement. I was still the same kid who, in college, had failed to find any theory of social contract plausible.

Knowledge is power. Those who have it are more powerful than those who do not. Those who define what counts as knowledge are the most powerful. They can make the rest of us crazy, learning disabled, or culturally deprived. Because knowledge is embedded in human interests, is constituted out of interest, those who define knowledge stand in a different relationship to knowledge from those who do not.

My central thesis in this book is that women stand in a different relationship to knowledge from men and that that makes every difference in education. In an androcentric culture, the intersubjective community to which all appeals are referred is a community from which women are either absent or represented as the objects of knowledge, rarely as its subjects. My arguments do not rest on any sort of *essential* femaleness or *essential* maleness. Nor do they rest on any sense of inevitability. Nor yet do they imply that men and women *ought* not to stand in difference relationships. On the contrary, I believe that the conversational model I adopt for this book and in my teaching requires the self-conscious production, acknowledgment, and celebration of difference. Difference, I argue, is the condition for the kind of connection demanded by a humane education. Instead, I find the representation of knowledge in institutionalized discourses which exclude from the domain of cognition, female subjectivity, to situate female and male, subject and object, self and other in structures of dominance and submission and inclusion and exclusion. Because knowledge and gender both are produced and reproduced against the background of available cultural representations, those who are excluded from or demeaned in those representations are at a distinct disadvantage. I find in these representations an implicit denial of difference, which denial represses the desire to merge with the Other, to assimilate the Other.

As I explore the general ethical questions of education, questions of knowledge and power, of authority and relationship, of what is owing to whom, as I explore the balance between the claims of the individual and the claims of community, I find that considerations of gender complicate all of these.

I began teaching in 1974 because it was the only job I could find. I had never studied education, had never thought about teaching at all. I followed a Miss Marple method of teaching. I had only my own experience and the intuitions that develop out of experience to rely on. I began my graduate study three years later at the University of Rochester. In my studies of curriculum theory there I came to understand my work as a teacher and a student to be con-textual, woven from threads of my history and culture. Studying William Pinar and Madeleine Grumet's work in educational autobiography, I inscribed my practice within a narrative that seemed sometimes to duplicate and sometimes to transform my practice. The text of my educational history taught me that the cultural conversation changes, indeed, those who participate in it. The stories I tell in the following chapters are stories of my conversations with my culture's past, and, therefore, with my own. They are also stories of my conversation with my present.

This book is autobiographical, even when it does not appear
to be. My conversations with Plato and Descartes and all the
others are autobiographical. They have as much to do with the
kitchen as with the office and the seminar room. My students, my
colleagues, and my friends wander in and out of these
conversations. Sometimes they help to embellish a theme;
sometimes they change the subject. Their presence keeps us from
getting stuck. Even when we talk to ourselves, we're talking to
someone else.

Any book about teaching is also about language. When we
teach we talk. The language we have learned to speak, like the
knowledge we have inherited, is androcentric. If we are not
careful, when we talk we express a male experience of the world.
If we are not careful, when we teach we help our students to
orient themselves to the axis of male experience. The Teacher, the
Poet, the Scientist, the Philosopher, the Lover, the nonspecific
"one," and all of the others whom we meet in school, try to turn
us toward that axis. A woman so oriented is disoriented. I do not
imply that women are less skillful or artful in expression. I simply
mean that because the anonymous competent speaker of our
institutionalized language is male, men and women have different
relationships to that language.

This is a feminist book, both in form and in content. In the
chapters that follow, I probe and probe again certain texts and
pursue certain fundamental problems to their origins in male
experience. I read my own experience, too, as having its origins in
male experience in order to teach myself to be careful and to
enlarge the possibilities of speaking. I try to find in that experience
and in the conversations that shape it, the possibility of new
expression. I use conversation as a model for pedagogy and as the
vehicle of theory. You will notice that I speak directly to other
women in places in this book. My conversations with them,
particularly my conversations with Madeleine Grumet, helped to
shape the practice that became this book. These *are* conversations.
Identity of position is not to be understood here. It is the
connection forged through conversation that permits and encour-
ages the consolidation of difference. Conversations lead on and
along a variety of paths.

Like Jane Marple, I tell stories to anchor my interpretations of
the conceptual problems I explore. I call frequently on novels. For
200 years the novel has been the document most accessible to

women and the most accessible document of women's lives. In employing it as I do here, I hope, in some measure, to feminize educational discourse. For the same reason I often concoct impertinent readings of sacred texts and treat seriously marginal ones. The topic of these stories and readings is my own pedagogical practice—even when it does not seem to be. Only if we can be playful with our most solemn prejudices can we develop a critical discourse that will enlarge our conversational circle and dislodge violence from educational practice. I offer this strategy as an alternative to androcentric "methodolatry." The use of narrative permits me to vary my distance from the object of my study. Oppressive practice depends on forms of expression organized oppositionally and hierarchically—presence-absence, intellect-emotion, public-private, self-other, objective-subjective, male-female. In each pair of an opposition, the first term is superior. Presence is superior to absence, reason to passion, and male to female. The narrative contests this structure at its root by refusing the domination inherent in such oppositions, by permitting us to hear what they conceal as well as what they express, and by preventing our collapse onto either term. Some contest patriarchy by reversing the order of the opposition such that "female" is read as superior. Such a move is still contained within the logocentric universe of patriarchal discourse and does not disturb the silence of the dominated term. A feminist discourse disturbs silence by demonstrating that each term depends on the other.

While this work is interdisciplinary in its choice of topics and in the material with which it deals, I employ feminist psychoanalytic theory in reading the stories I tell. With the help of psychoanalytic theory I come to see how difference is produced in culture, and I discover ways of insisting on the production of difference in order to expand our universes of discourse and open up the cultural conversation. I also come to see the vital link between difference and connection and the tenuousness of the apparently obvious opposition between difference and sameness. These readings transform my relationship to the language of my practice. I bring to my readings and stories questions of authority and correctness, of the relationship of the reader to the experience of reading, and of the sexual domination implicit in the humanist tradition. I attempt to reconfigure the topology of these questions.

I approach educational experience as a text both variously and similarly available to all who encounter it.

The second part of my title, "Teaching in the Patriarchal Wilderness," has a long lineage. In *Criticism in the Wilderness* Geoffrey Hartmann said that all criticism takes place in a wilderness. Elaine Showalter borrowed the title from Hartmann, adding the word "Feminist."

My title claims one lineage and contests another, even as it acknowledges it claim. The image of the wilderness works for me in a number of ways. First is the obvious sense that to teach as a female teacher is to teach in an androcentric wilderness. The task of feminist criticism in education is to make the place fit for women to live in. I also claim the title with a sense of ironic appropriation. The wilderness in patriarchy is symbolic of the powerful devouring mother. At the same time, in American literature men go to the wilderness to get away from women and feminine civilization. Triumph in the wilderness redeems the individual masculine soul. But women can claim the wilderness too, can speak there and read there as women speak and read. And many have. This book is also a conversation with them; it was made possible by our conversations. Feminist theory and pedagogy both assert connections. This is a book of connections.

Elaine Showalter urges us to move beyond the revisionist mode of feminist criticism. "Affirmative action criticism," she says, criticism contained within the universe of patriarchal logocentrism does not lead to transformed practice. This is not to deny the contributions of revisionist criticism. But it cannot lead to alternative practice, because it depends for its meaning on androcentric models of criticism. Showalter argues that a peculiarly feminist practice must be woman centered. It must be gynocritical. Gynocriticism does not replace androcentric models. There are still male readers, after all, and no one is recommending that they become female readers. A feminized criticism enlarges and enriches the conversational circle by admitting women not just as objects but also as subjects, readers, writers, and critics. It enriches the conversation by naming and admitting female experience, by breaking the silence enjoined on the feminine wilderness by patriarchal logocentrism. Nothing is lost but rigidity if a reading demonstrates the way in which practice obeys the imperatives of patriarchy.[1]

In his summary of feminist theory in literature, Jonathan

Culler asks us to suppose that the informed reader of a work is a woman and that her sex makes all the difference. Reviewing the work of Showalter and others, Culler finds three moments of reading as a woman. In the first moment criticism is thematic, appeals to the reader's experience, and argues a continuity between her experience of texts and her experience in the social world. The second moment is the one in which the woman reader understands that she has not been reading as a woman. She understands that she has been subdued and seduced by the text. She has been led to identify with male interests against her own. This is the moment at which the presumed gender neutrality of knowledge is challenged. In the third moment, the woman reader discovers that her own notions of the work have been tied to, and even complicit with, the male's. The female critic's job is to explore alternatives to methods, assumptions, and goals which preserve male authority.[2]

My intention in telling my stories and constructing my readings is to inscribe androcentric educational practices within a larger textual system. I do that by proceeding through the moments of feminist criticism discovering my own practice to be embedded in an androcentric universe. At the same time I find the stories of my practice in that universe to contain the possibility of talk that opens up the conversational circle. The textual reinterpretations enacted in the following pages redeem the contexts and subtexts excluded from logocentric thinking. They redeem difference and connection and interrogate sameness and merging.

Among our common stock of cultural images there are many teachers. They should teach us something. But when I look to them I do not find myself. I am no good and wise Mr. Chips. I am no artist gentleman who withers the boys with a solemn look. I am impressed when people write of the famous men who have been their professors. The cigarette ash tumbling headlong down a worn sportsjacket; the impressive voice and heedless courage of the scholar preforming a problem for his public; the wit, the gentle sarcasm, the charisma of the scholar who allows us a glimpse of the grace of the life of the mind—I am enchanted and entranced by these figures. I am bemused by the professor who insists that it is the student's job to understand him and not his job to make himself understood, and by the student who says, "He's so brilliant no one can understand him." I do not find myself there.

A couple of years ago one of my very good female students came to my office with a question about a class assignment. It was a small question and quickly dealt with. She thanked me, gathered her books and papers, and began talking—about her family, her roommate, her dog, her boyfriend. Finally she seemed ready to leave, but still clearly had something else on her mind. She shifted her weight from leg to leg, fiddled with the corner of her notebook, asked me what other courses I was teaching, where I had gone to college. Then, she came out with it. Not meeting my eyes, she said, "Are you married?" Without giving me a chance to reply, she hurried on, "We were wondering—Sue and I—and we thought you couldn't be married, because you always have all your own ideas and things."

The force of the phrase "having all my own ideas and things" nearly knocks the breath out of me. So much is insinuated. I am a teacher, and I always have all my own ideas and things. I am also a wife, a daughter, a sister, and friend, to some I suppose, an enemy. I read and I write and I garden and I bake. All of these things surface in this book because all of them have everything to do with my being a teacher and having all of my own ideas and things. That is what this book is about. It took shape in conversation, and in it I attempt to talk back to the women whose talk has been important to me. In a sense this book is a report or a reproduction of conversations.

I worry that my male friends and colleagues will feel slighted and excluded. Buy any book about women is also about men. We share the worlds we make. Virginia Woolf once asked us to imagine that all we had ever known about men we had known through their relationships with women. We can easily imagine how lopsided our view of the world would be. We now know that all we have seen and heard of women has given us a lopsided view of the world. In reading women's work and in reading it as women, we may identify themes and strategies that will enable us to claim our stories and make a narrative habitation in the wilderness of women's silence. In such a place men and women might speak together.

The organization of these chapters is circular. This book begins and ends in the present moment. I contrast this organization to a Socratic dialogue, our usual model for conversation in pedagogy. I do not start with your false premises and ask you to discard them for my more adequate substitutes.

Unlike Socrates and his friends and lovers who come together to dispute a problem, and then, having solved it, disperse, and go their separate ways, I choose to emphasize position and approach rather than destination. I choose to contest patriarchal models of authority.

1

Representing and Representation in Educational Theory

> . . . Even if I could answer the
> question for myself, the answer
> would apply only to me and not to
> you. The only advice, indeed, that
> one person can give another about
> reading is to take no advice, to
> follow your own instincts, to use
> your own reason, to come to your
> own conclusions. If this is agreed
> between us, then I feel at liberty to
> put forward a few ideas and sug-
> gestions because you will not allow
> them to fetter that independence
> that is the most important quality a
> reader can possess.
> —Virginia Woolf, *How Should One
> Read A Book?*

How do we describe what we do? Why do we do what we do?
How do we think about what we do? How are we implicated in
what we know? What are the institutions like through which our
knowledge is formed? How are we implicated in those institutions? What actions are required by our knowledge? For what are
we responsible and in what does our freedom consist? Who are
these knowing subjects and where in the world do they find
themselves? What is represented in our knowledge, and how do
we represent it? These questions are fundamental to educational
theory and pedagogical practice.

As we proceed through these questions, we make stories or
narratives of educational experience, stories having the communal

1

pedagogical force of myth. These are stories of our individuality as that is achieved through the languages of the public worlds constituted by our disciplines and by the institutions within which the disciplines are organized. They are also stories of our own mastery of the conventions of the narratives that structure our disciplines and institutions. But each of us must decide these questions for herself. Each must tell her own story, and the power to do so is a central aim of education. It is also the central problematic. Discourses in any field define the stories that can be expressed; they permit certain stories to unfold, and they forbid others. Discourse communities may be exclusive. Feminist stories contest exclusion. Virginia Woolf's search for a female sentence expresses that knowledge. The male sentence, she knew, forbade the female story.[3]

Teacher's Stories: Narratives of Teaching, Speaking, and Reading

In a democracy, education should prepare each of us to tell our own stories. Discourses through which we might shape these stories must, then, be available to us. In the power of our own voices telling our own stories, our inclinations to freedom are achieved. In our free speakings we freely choose participation in the cultural and political life our stories sustain. We learn to tell our stories in conversation with the stories we are told. We learn to speak, and we learn to read, and part of learning to speak and to read is learning the narrative conventions and acquiring the values of the discourse communities within which those stories have significance. We inhabit discourses. In learning the rules for speaking and reading, we learn to judge those matters which help us to decide how we ought to live our lives. The subtext of any educational story is a moral one because discursive rules are moral rules defining and limiting relationships.

Educational researchers in this decade have increasingly concerned themselves with teacher and student narratives. We have become sensible of and sensitive to the lore that has always been part of the stock in trade of the novelist—that the way a person tells the story of her life and her work, the motives which she attributes to herself, and the significances of her tales of her relationships with others which elude and tantalize, is finally what her work as a teacher is all about.

Much of this research reports consistent themes and tensions in the stories teachers tell. Over and over again we read narratives heavy with ambivalence about authority; over and over again we read tales of conflicting aims of selves and institutions. We are accustomed to reading stories of teachers who understand the imperatives of self to be undermined by the imperatives of community membership. The conflict at the heart of these narratives perhaps defines the conflict at the heart of education, or at least at the heart of an educational project described by all who take it as their own—liberatory. In these liberatory stories, education is conceived as empowering. This conception comes smash up against the fact that the education we receive is one which assimilates all to a single version of humanity and reality, a version predicated on the imperatives of patriarchy. In this version, a romantic and isolationist self finds *himself,* besieged and beleaguered by a community which threatens to swallow him whole. We may call this the standard story in the genre. This standard story is grounded in a myth of the storyteller's relationship to language, a relationship to language which places the woman storyteller in an ambiguous position. For the position which she must take up as storyteller is one from which she, as speaker, as teller, must be absent. According to psychoanalytic theory, the infant's first representations are of the absent mother; they are substitutes for the source of nourishment and compensations for her absence. The child first vocalizes to express its frustration and to control its mother's movement. Representation and discourse are built on the first opposition the child encounters—the opposition between self and other. Otherness and absence are said to be the first knowledge and the basis of discourse. Discourse then defines relationship. Storytelling, the representation of an absent object, is the way in which we compensate for the mother's otherness.

French psychoanalytic theory as practiced by Lacan and his followers and critics, presumes that speaking is an act of desire, sometimes a compulsive act of desire, the object of which always and necessarily eludes the speaker. To tell a story is to control an absent object. The original absent object is the mother. The present object is the separated and abandoned self. To tell a story is to assert a present self by constructing substitutes for the absent Other.

That human existence is pervasively tragic, Freud claimed, is a consequence of original loss and absence. Lack and the desire to replace it are what define human existence. Therefore, speakers define their presence against the mother's absence for it is only with her absence that the self is known. Freud said that to enter the world is to leave behind an experience of "oceanic oneness." Need does not exist because lack does not exist. The newborn infant knows no hunger, no cold, no wet diapers. "His majesty the baby," as Freud called the infant, is ruler of all he surveys. According to Lacan, the original human relationship, that between mother and child, is an imaginary one. Its register is the image. The original mother-child dyad is unmediated by language or anything else. The child extends the mother, and her look completes him. In her gaze the world is given. Finally, though, the mother looks away. The world, in the form of the father, steps in. The rule of patriarchy claims the child from its mother. Its register is language. The child is alone, fragmented, as the world is fragmented. At the moment that the mother looks away the child is lost to himself. The maternal body, the source of all pleasure, is withheld; it belongs to another. And yet the child remains dependent for all of his pleasure on that which he may not have. He is thrown into a world defined by him by his desire for reunion, his awareness of his dreadful separateness, his knowledge that the powerful father forbids reunion, and his fear of the consequences of his desire. His life is measured by a simultaneous need to merge with and disengage from his mother. The child speaks. His only compensation for the enormous developmental task ahead of him is the acquired power of symbolic representation. With symbols he replaces the abandoning mother. At first the child may represent the literal mother, calling her into presence in his mind even when she is absent. Later symbolic representations are aspects of these early representations of the mother. They come to stand for an Other who is like, in some way, the original Other.

Children begin to acquire language at about the same time that they become aware of sexual difference. The mark of that difference is, of course, the phallus. The father, who has taken the mother from the child, who has forbidden the union which the child so desperately desires, possesses both phallus and mother. Because the mother does not possess the phallus, the phallus becomes not just a physical characteristic of some persons and not others, not just the mark of sexual differentiation, but the symbol of all difference. The possessor of the phallus interrupts, breaks communion. At the same time that the phallus stands symbolically for the mother's absence, it becomes a symbol of power, the power to possess the mother. But only symbolically, for the fundamental prohibition of patriarchal rule is the rule against incest. So the child may never possess the object of his desire. Even he who possesses the phallus is denied the original object. He can only generate symbolic substitutes. One day he may possess an object like the mother. According to this theory, the fact of symbolic language requires unfulfillable desire, requires an absence for which the generation of symbols, the representation of she whose presence is desired, compensates. Language, storytelling, provides a symbolic return of the lost object.

The daughter's position is different. She lacks the phallus. But equally important, and Freud missed the significance of this although Lacan did not, the daughter is not different from the mother, from the original object of desire.[4] Nevertheless, she must enter the father's symbolic order. Unlike her brother whose entry into the symbolic order follows on his awareness of difference from his mother, the daughter maintains a primary identification with her mother. She is *like* her mother. But the symbolic order which claims her is predicated first on the fact of differentiation, of difference from the mother, and later on a need to maintain that difference. The female child confronts a heroic task. For entry into the father's order demands the absence of that object which she is like. In a sense, entry into the father's order is predicated on her own absence.

Lacan's revision of Freud's story appropriates to the second knowledge the status of foundation and denies the child's first knowledge. Lacan's reading of Freud does indeed describe the institutionalized story of epistemology in patriarchal discourse. This story is revisionist history denying as it does, epistemological status to the child's first knowledge—the knowledge of connection to the maternal. The story denies the existence of the self first given in the maternal gaze and appropriates consciousness to the knowledge of separation. Separation becomes the foundation of knowledge, and substitution and domination the conditions of consciousness. In this story women are excluded form language *as women* because language substitutes for the original female absence. In this story women are the objects of language and knowledge, but women can never be known directly. Women are ever deferred along a chain of symbolic substitutes. Can we claim to have knowledge of the prelapsarian state, can we claim knowledge of connection? Such knowledge appears to call for another (or Other) discourse(s)—discourse(s) which would permit stories that reclaim the knowledge excluded by the institutionalized discourses of Freud and Lacan and their followers.

In her study of the literary strategies of nineteenth century female writers, Margaret Homans details the implications of sexual difference for women's writing with respect to what she calls Lacan's "myth of language."[5] Her investigation of women's writing posits a prior knowledge and brings us to an examination of women's writing as discourse that expresses that knowledge. She argues that there are distinct male and female voices in literature, distinct registers, perhaps, which she refers to as figurative and literal. The distinction, as Homans draws it, enables her to claim epistemic status for the original connection and to explore the consequences of that knowledge for women. The woman, Homans says, maintains a literal identification with the maternal body, that first source of the world, of knowledge, of pleasure, pain, and desire. For this reason, as Lacan noted, the experience that propels the child into the linguistic register is different for males and females. Their relationship to language is different. For the male, the experience is one of total loss. The woman's exile from the maternal body is not, however, entire. The male speaks to fill a void. He speaks to make the world which once was made in the maternal gaze. His discourse denies a forbidden connection—a forbidden knowledge. But what if the speaker is female?

The history of our culture, Homans argues, is told from the point of view of a male speaker. This is a speaker who enters a discourse of substitution and denial. To enter our cultural traditions is to acquire a collection of representations predicated on the literal absence of the female. This means two things: to speak requires, ironically, the female's silence, and to know ourselves as women is to know ourselves through symbolic representations of male desire. How then is a woman to speak, to write, or to paint? Homans' readings of several female works offer evidence that this question is a central one in certain women's novels. To tell a story is to create a figurative representation. But if the teller is a woman, hers is the literal body for which representation substitutes. Virginia Woolf searched for a female sentence. Homans has shown us where and how to look for it. While Lacan suggests that woman *qua* woman cannot speak, Homans demonstrates that she has spoken. So have others whom we will meet in these pages. The primary strategy for women's writing has been one of resubstitution or, perhaps, resymbolization. The female strategy is one which literalizes, reembodies the figure. It transforms the figure by fastening it to a literal object. *Wuthering Heights* is a marvelous example of resymbolization of the figure which turns it back to the literal object. The insistent presence of the landscape around the heights, the figure of the house, assert the connection to the maternal body even as that body is denied in the written figures of patriarchy. The woman who speaks or writes as a woman moves back and forth between the poles of the literal and the figurative. She refuses to lose the body to its representations. But discourse is not the body; a story is not mimetic. A story is transformative. And the mode of transformation and its effect are central to feminist theory and to feminist teaching.

In a paper on concept validity and autobiographical research, Madeleine Grumet offers another way of thinking about the tension between the figurative and the literal. Educational research and teaching, since teaching is a form of research, must shift between two discursive modes. These two modes she identifies as mimetic and transformative. The two modes are identified with two forms of representation—narrative and theoretical. We may think of these as related to Homans' literal-figurative distinction. Mimetic discourse is associated with art while theoretical discourse is associated with science. In the one we enact or reenact our relation to the world. In the other we transform that relation. In the one we find the world; it is present to us. In the other we make that world an object of inquiry in order to transform it. The world is literal; it takes place literally, Grumet says. But we must not surrender to it, any more than we can surrender to the maternal gaze which gave us the world in the first place. Nor can we lose it in our figures. If our teaching is to transform the world then we must, as Grumet says, let the world in.[6] Art is not strictly mimetic, though. As discourse it does not mirror the world; it asserts the world. An enactment is a resymbolization.

These questions of language, representation, and narrative are pertinent to teaching. To teach, much of the time, is to tell. Certainly one can teach only a limited number of things without speaking. When we teach, we participate in the public worlds constituted by our disciplines and by the institutions and discourses within which these are organized. We do so through acts of representation and narration. We tell stories.

The word 'representation' designates facts, explanations, assertions, reproductions, and symbolizations. Deriving from that usage is one wherein 'representation' refers to the state of standing in for another for some purpose, either of one thing for another, one person for another, a thing for a person, or a person for a thing. But historically ancillary to any of these meanings is the sense in which a representation is an act of the imagination which brings into presence or which brings one to some privilege or state. A narrative may be a representation in any of these senses, as may a teaching. A feminist educational project insists on the primacy of the gender of story, of the teller's relationship to language in these representations. Our question is whether representation necessarily transforms the object of desire into a substitute for desire and whether it demands denial of connection.

The Gender of Educational Stories

For our students we are representatives of our disciplines and institutions, both in respect of what or who we are and in respect of the representations we make. We bring into presence the customs and content of our disciplines and institutions. We explain, assert, reproduce, and symbolize them. When we teach we speak; we make stories. We represent through narration. We stand in for the grand theories and sublime forms that are our culture's transformations of original mimetic experience. When we ask the questions I urge us to ask, we interrogate our own representations; we transform them. We are critics of ourselves as represented. We are critics of our representations. We construct narrations on our narrations. In the Lacanian story, a woman teacher is an odd creature—one who represents as an actor represents. She is like one of Shakespeare's boys dressed up as a girl masquerading as a boy.

For women teachers, representation is problematic in all of its senses if discourse denies the knowledge of connection, or if it forbids the knowledge of that connection. The discursive rules and narrative conventions according to which we designate facts, explain, assert, reproduce, and symbolize are conventions acquired in a second language, the language of the fathers. This claim supposes, of course, that we have a first language. If we have, it has been long forgotten. What we stand in for or substitute for is also problematic. For the language in which we represent is a language predicated on our absence, or on the absence of the original object which we resemble. We stand in for traditions and conventions, judgments, and values which are not our own—traditions, conventions, judgments, and values in which our worth, our integrity, our separateness are contested. We represent, stand in for, those traditions within which we live as exiles. These traditions are the houses our brothers have built for themselves in their exile from the maternal body. They are at home there. We are political and epistemological refugees. In the sense in which our representations bring into presence or bring one to a state of privilege, we bring into presence our own absence because the privilege is the privilege of the separate self who is the foundation of knowledge. The privilege to which we bring others is a privilege predicated on our observing the quarantine imposed on the dark continent of femininity by the Freudian-Lacanian myth of discourse and epistemology. The relatives who stayed behind there must fend for themselves.

The word "narrative" first appears in English in 1748 with the publication of *Clarissa*.[7] The novel is about many things: property, patriarchal authority, the conduct of women and the obligations of men. At the center of the tale is Clarissa's rape, a rape for which she claims responsibility and willingly bears the guilt because she entered into correspondence with the scheming Lovelace. Lovelace is a master of writing as well as of all the masculine pursuits and vices. It is just Clarissa's innocent body and literary sensibility which he must mark with his penis/pen.[8] She is quite literally a bearer of the word. Among her other suitors, and the one insisted upon by her family, is the thoroughly unattractive Mr. Solmes, who, as Brownstein observes, writes indifferently and spells badly. Through letters, Lovelace persuades Clarissa, under his protection, to leave her odious family and escape her marriage to Solmes. He takes her to a brothel where other women assist him in drugging and raping her. As women teachers bearing the word of patriarchal culture, we find ourselves both in Clarissa's position and in that of Lovelace's assistants. We seduce our female students with the same stories that seduced us, the stories of our cultural heritage. That is one story of women's teaching. The feminist project in education is one of revision. We speak to tell another story. We speak to transform and to refigure our fathers' figures. We contest the appropriation of discourse itself to the knowledge of male separation.

Madeleine Grumet has represented to us the bittersweetness and the irony of women teaching. She tells a story in which women teaching is like women mothering, but unlike. The stories are similar in that both mother and teacher must "deliver" their conceptions, made vital and nourished in private, to the public world of the fathers. The stories diverge in that the female teacher acts simultaneously as both mother and daughter. She delivers and is delivered (in a sense has delivered herself) to a public world which offers comfort only in a jealous privacy, a privacy dependent on difference denied and desire deferred. But we recalled the private worlds from which we are exiles in the public world of our loneliness. With curtains drawn and lamps shaded we sometimes looked back through the scrapbooks we managed to hide on our persons, in our clothing, in our forced emigration from the dark continent of femininity.[9] But we are, nonetheless, our fathers' daughters, too.

The fragments, photos, and clippings in those scrapbooks stirred something unnamed in us, having no referents in the language of the fathers. They evoked memories that were not quite memories, having less solidity than re-membrance, being something other than substitution. And so we whispered the bits of stories we could gather from these vague stirrings and evocations and listened for the resonances beneath the public tales that others told for the timbres and nuances, the rhythms and codes that might help us to complete the tale of our exile and settle in this wilderness. At first our stories simply named our exile, heavy with loss and populated by figures of anxiety.

Since we began talking to one another, women scholars have regularly referred to the feeling of being inappropriate, of having missed something crucial. ("I must have been absent the day they taught that.") In philosophy courses, especially those in ethics, we learned that our concerns were irrelevant in adjudicating justice and injustice. Motives, provocations, alternatives, etc. are as much beside the point as we ourselves. We learned these lessons and became very good at principles. We learned to keep what was in our hearts in silence. In psychology classes we found ourselves deviant. We learned of our fear of success, of our motivational problems, our dependency (excessive), our timidity, and our irrationality. In science we aligned ourselves with the fathers of reason against our common enemy—Mother Nature. In art and literature we found ourselves excluded or deformed, victimized or victimizer, but we understood why the heroes must leave us. We tried to be more like them. We liked Nick Carraway better than Daisy Buchanan, and Gatsby at least had dash. Nick could tell the truth; Daisy was its object, and Gatsby, we learn, the real creator of the object—a truth discoverable, though, only by the lonely teller of the tale. In the domain of educational theory we found ourselves missing (the teacher is *he* who attempts to achieve desirable ends through rational means). As apt students we believed. We were divided from ourselves by the tales of our fathers. We were their accomplices.

But we did begin talking to one another. And as we talked we began to inquire into the names of things, to understand the responsibility involved in naming, and to evaluate the moral implications of the relationships embedded in our acts of signification. We came to produce different kinds of narrative. We began to understand the fathers' power over signification. We began to understand that the power to signify for us, as women, is a power granted to a surrogate. We began to understand that we are representatives of the father's order, an order in which women are represented only as lack or deformity. Our conversations provoked serious questions about our own work and our implication in the institutions and disciplines which silenced us even as we represented those institutions and disciplines. We came to see that we brought into presence, stood in for, that which denied and deformed us. Talking together we learned to name the exile and to claim our knowledge of connection. We learned to forge new claims and to work them out in a discourse of affiliation.

As narratives having the instructive force of myth, stories of educational experience, the texts which we make of our lives in classrooms, teach us what it means to be knowing creatures, what it means to know ourselves as selves. They teach us about the relationships between cognition and emotion, between reason and passion, between the mind and the body, between epistemology and politics. Finally, they help us to negotiate the tension between the individual and the community, a tension never resolved or resolvable because of the fact of difference, a tension which indeed is the subtext of all educational narratives.

To be educated in a democracy means to possess the stories through which we acquire our individual identities as members of our communities. These claims do not originate with feminists. But our educational narratives, narratives saturated with the anxiety of patriarchy, undermine the democratic educational project. Even as they are enlarged to include women and other minorities, they do so by denying the power of the different voice, the authenticity of its tales, forbidding them a place in the tradition. I note an irony: while the history of education has been in one sense a history of inclusion, the stories that we have learned to tell are stories of exclusion. The more successful we have been as students, scholars, and teachers, the greater has been our active participation in our own exclusion. Martha Quest's life in Doris Lessing's *Children of Violence* novels, is an example of a series of exclusions and self-alienations. *The Golden Notebook,* also written by Lessing, is a story of exile too. Anna Wulf can no longer write and can no longer participate in her life as a successful writer because she is alienated in her work, exiled perhaps. *Hunger of Memory,* Richard Rodriquez's autobiography, expresses the peculiar pain of inclusion. He talks about the delight of a mother in her fair-skinned children, children who might more easily assimilate. A searing memory recalls the scholarship boy on a summer construction job, cut off by all of the habits of his training, from the other Mexican-Americans. At the same time, the scholarship boy is no more at home at the meetings of the Modern Language Association. To be successful in these public worlds, to be included in them, many of us are required to discard our histories. I remember being pleased as a young woman to be told that I thought more like a man than a woman. "Woman thinking" appeared, in fact, to be a contradiction. It is not that women can't think—it is simply that we cannot think *as women.* If we would think, we must think in the voice of the culture in which we are subdued.

Since the Enlightenment, the educational project has been assimilated to a gentlemanly search for a rational basis for human conduct. In the search for a rational basis, all of those sentiments, dispositions, and characteristics we have come to associate with the feminine have acquired negative value. We might go so far as to say that all of those thoughts and emotions which could not be expressed within a story of rationality narrowly construed have been relegated to the feminine.

Through feminist criticism we began to explore the dark continent to which our thoughts and feelings, and the knowledge of connection once possessed by male and female both, had been exiled. We began to deconstruct our habits of reading and storytelling, habits which have become habits of the heart and mind. In unsealing the dark continent we let out of quarantine all of those things contained by reason and principle. We began to ask what if . . .? What if our common sense notions of authority, responsibility, and power were different? We began to make relevant the irrelevant, and we began to imagine a different world of different selves. The world we began to imagine is one wherein possibilities of action and discourse are expanded rather than contracted, where difference promises fullness and range of expression. We located the literal body beneath its figurative substitutes. I am not the first to have noted that a feminist consciousness disturbs the bodily sites onto which the conventions of educational narratives are grafted. Doris Lessing's dialectical imagination, perhaps nowhere so powerfully at work as in *The Golden Notebook*, doubles discourse and the worlds expressed in it and invites our participation in a conversation that neither excludes nor dominates. Saul's gift of a sentence to the previously silenced Anna enables a story in which male and female and female and female connect in language rather than separate: "The two women were together in the room."

Feminist educational theory is a tricky business. In educating we transmit a tradition in which women are silent, in which we are, at best, footnotes to the relevant facts. As teachers we represent a culture which has demanded, as the price of the privilege to represent, our conspiracy with a heritage that privileges only a few. We have learned to present ourselves as the genderless "author," "artist," or "scientist." We have learned to quell any doubts we may have had about our right to so present ourselves, to speak in the voice of authority—the tradition—and to compete with our male colleagues for scarce academic resources. We have been careful to hunch our bodies in shameful secrecy as we walked the corridors of our departments for fear that someone would notice we were in drag.

Feminist Narratives: Telling, Teaching, and Theory

To acknowledge our relationship to our traditions as one simply of subordinate to dominant is disingenuous. These are the traditions in which we learned to speak. We can no more refuse to participate in them (nor is it clear to me that we should want to) than we can represent them as figures of ourselves. We are scientists, social scientists, philosophers, psychologists, humanists, artists, teachers, and writers. Moreover, we cherish our cultural heritage. And we must admit that somehow we have managed to bring ourselves to presence through those very traditions which first establish and then compensate for our absence. The task I see for feminist theory in education just now is one of making conversation with our professions and with our history within them. We can theorize our vulnerability as practitioners of our disciplines and as teachers, speak our exile and, in doing so, resettle our disciplinary communities.

Many women at the present moment *are* describing and theorizing education in modes of representation which inquire systematically into the names of things in order to create new things, new stories. These scholars perform narrative acts in which we all can converse as ourselves, in which we make ourselves present. These stories are not figured on the absence and separation predicated as conditions of knowledge in the Freudian myth.

Freud despaired of ever understanding what women want. That was because he could not imagine a creature unlike himself. Those women to whom he could speak, female members of the psychoanalytic community, he simply assimilated to the masculine. They were, he said, more masculine than feminine. Insofar as they were not, they were, they were told, part of the problem and could be no help at all in discovering the way in which the feminine is produced.[10] Equality—of access or of outcome—is not the issue here. To be equal in the patriarchal scheme is to be as good as, the same as, the dominant male. We women do not want equality if equality means equal access to the superior position in a structure of domination and submission, in an order sustained by absence. We do not want the power to oppress, to maim, and to silence. If we women are to find our voices, we must insist on describing and claiming the difference produced in experience and on naming and claiming the original connection denied and forbidden in patriarchal discourse.

Nel Noddings and Jane Roland Martin, each in their different ways, place women and those claims associated with the feminine neatly into educational discourse, successfully reconfiguring the topography of the educational narrative.[11] Theirs are stories in which we come to ourselves in a moment of recognizing that those who are included are as grievously maimed, as oddly shaped and grotesque, as those who are excluded. When our narratives of educational experience become genuinely inclusive, then the ways in which we choose to look at our practice and the ways that we meet those whom we encounter in our practice necessarily change. The worlds we imagine in our practice become more hospitable because they are more spacious.

In an essay describing, criticizing, and potentially transforming the education of women philosophers, Elizabeth Young-Bruehl elaborates the narratives of Noddings and Martin.[12] She describes to us the haunting of Western philosophy by an image of a polis of the mind in which one part of the mind—the rational—defined as one truth and one representational process, rules the others. The rule of the rational, the rule of the one over the many, she speculates, is the source of oppression and repression. The preeminence of the modes of assimilation and analogy in this image of the mind is in service of repression. But what is repressed in the unconscious always returns. She cleverly employs this insight of Freud's to develop an alternative image.

Young-Bruehl exposes assimilation and analogy as the dominant modes of patriarchal reason and as representational modes which enact a denial and devalorization of difference, specifically of feminine difference. Female experience must be assimilated to male experience, and women must be understood to be *like* men, just as immigrants must be "Americanized." *Male experience* is the uncontested model of experience against which all experience is to be understood and judged. Freud's female colleagues are worthy only because they are more masculine than feminine and a splitting headache for Freud insofar as they are feminine.

Difference defies the order of the male standard, the rule of the one, precisely because male representational modes are strategies which must either assimilate all subjectivity to that of the singular self or deny the subjectivity of the other by banishing that subjectivity to the dark continent of mystery and multiplicity, to an unrepresentable language.[13] In Young-Bruehl's story, our psychological processes are in conversation and the unitary subject, the ruler of all he infers, is exposed as a figure of patriarchal mythology. To expose his mythic function is to begin the critique of the rule of the rational. The conversation among primary and secondary processes which she imagines as the material out of which the story of the polis of the mind is woven is radically democratic and antiauthoritarian. Pedagogy as conversation reinstitutes the democratic mind.

We must take care, though, to avoid a sentimentalization of connection, of community, and of feeling. We must take care to avoid appropriating connection, community, and feeling to a sense of something that is *essentially* feminine. Young-Bruehl does avoid these traps, and she eschews the exile of reason from the conversation. If we say that the original knowledge is knowledge of connection, we are committed neither to claiming it as privileged knowledge, to asserting the essential femininity of that knowledge, nor to assimilating knowledge to mimesis and situating it strictly within the realm of the unspeakable maternal. The democratic mind, the mind in conversation with both the fact of separation *and* the fact of connection is one in which neither sense nor sensibility stands tyrant. Feminist theorists celebrate the multidimensional and multivalent possibilities of representation, both literal and figurative. What women want, indeed what we must have if education is to enable us to act for and as ourselves, to represent ourselves and our experience, is not a privileged story, but our own story. Our stories are continually constructed and reconstructed through our conversations with each other and with our cultural heritage. They are produced in our experience, and they produce that experience. They are not expressions of a unitary and fixed subject.

All feminist scholarship in education listens to and tries to reproduce the nuances and inflections of the female voice as it is produced in gendered experience. We try to explore with Virginia Woolf the female sentence. Such a sentence will cleave the silence, will break it against the voice of experience, and in breaking it, cleave/heal the cleft forced by patriarchal modes of representation. Our explorations will show us that the dark continent of femininity is not the realm of unreason, disorder and silence. These are not easy explorations. Our very real social and institutional power inheres in our fluency in the language and conventions of patriarchy, however much our fluency may be the fluency of the clever exile or of Freud's female colleagues as he hears them.

While we appear successfully to have decoupled femininity from biology, femininity seems still to remain a psychological construct, a signifier for a set of psychological dispositions and capacities. Psychological essentialism gets us no further than biological essentialism, though. Our interest in developing a feminist theory of education, I think, goes far beyond that of honoring biological or psychological difference. We mean not simply to describe a set of psychological postulates about femininity, and then, because we are liberal democrats, to argue that they be held in high regard. Our interest is in reappropriating, reclaiming for all of those postulates of femininity, biological as well as psychological, a central place in epistemological and moral discourse as well as in political discourse. Femininity includes modes of knowing, representing, and judging. The feminine has existential, epistemological, and moral referents in men and women alike, and if represented will benefit men and women alike. The muteness of any deprives of resonance the voices of all.

Conversation:
Reading and Interpreting Our Texts of Teaching

It is easy, if uncomfortable, to succumb to the enchantments of hyperrationalism and fall into to the sleep of reason. It may be tempting to retreat into silence or to speak in tongues in the frenzy of the Sibyl. Entering and sustaining conversation is tricky business. We are only beginning to learn strategies for carrying out the negotiation and for making the required shifts between poles of experience and discourse. A feminist theory of education is no abstract business, no pure and uncontaminated seeing, no "immaculate perception," to borrow a delightful term from Clifford Geertz. A feminist theory is a theory of practice and a practice of theory in which the acts of theorizing and practicing are continually re-presented as artifacts of the unrepresented. These are transformations through which presence contradicts absence by enlarging experience and naming desire.

As I sit here writing, I think about the act of writing and the act of writing within a tradition of women teachers. And I think about a language for talking about that tradition, a tradition of silence. We naturally claim a patrimony, but what do we claim from our mothers? "Matrimony" refers only to the relation between a husband and wife. Very well. Let us see what we can make of a marriage as we try to make a heritage. Virginia Woolf taught us, after all, that poetry must have a mother and a father both.

Again and again the voice haunts women's writing. The voice of our patrimony is too distant, too deep, and too loud for us to pitch our own to. As we work through our histories we find ourselves over and over again reviewing, rehearsing, and revising the stories of our patrimony as we try to move ourselves to a critical location which is neither near nor far but both at once. We are learning to read all over again as we learn to speak and to speak together. Part of the strategy of our reading is one of making the marginal central. In our new readings we displace the oppositions through which we learned to read as good students and good daughters. We challenge logocentrism by producing multiple readings. Virginia Woolf fantasized that just as there may be more than two sexes in the body, so may there be more than two in the mind. In the virtuous mind, the rule of the one is displaced in the speaking together of all the sexes. In such a mind the literal present is as valued as its figurative compensation.

Feminism issues from the Enlightenment as surely as we daughters know our fathers, as clearly as we have learned to recite the tales of their lineage. Its categories are ours and our experience has been produced through that heritage. At the same time, feminism contests the Enlightenment by resisting assimilation to the rule of the one and deferring from a singular and closed rational discourse. The body is asserted in feminism and the pleasure of the everyday instituted as an object of reflection and daily experience as a reflective act.

There are artists and writers and teachers and scientists and philosophers. There are texts and theorems and syllogisms and styles. There are also cooking pots which bubble over onto stoves while you think about the essay you're writing. I write, therefore my stove's a mess. There are students who do and don't care about you, about whom you care or do not. There are men, and there are women, and it is more advantageous to be one than the other. Which you choose to be depends on what you want or on what you have learned to want. "Education is an ideological apparatus of the capitalist state." There are clothes dryers that go on the fritz and burn up all of your husband's underwear two days before you leave for a conference. How could things be much worse in a socialist state?

Education is something that happens in rooms where people feel empty or happy, and it is a thing that happens between and among people as they learn to speak together. I have had an education, but I cannot tell you where I keep it. It is just here, in what I say, just there in what I claim and acknowledge. There are words and there are things, and sometimes we say what we mean, and sometimes we say what we can. There are great books, and philosophy is fine. And a woman teacher cannot but be ambivalent about the whole business.

It's five o'clock. In October in this part of the world the atmosphere is lit with a certain special sadness made lively by a promise. The mist makes patches on my office window. I look around and between them to watch the flock of geese moving away from here. And I am someone's daughter who has cared for other women's children. And mothers lose their children as surely as children lose their mothers. But something is found or can be. Not as compensation but as enlargement, desire deferred and desire made possible. Deliberately I leave these thoughts as I find them.

Our representations of educational experience, both our own and those of others promise no grand conclusions. Their gift is a gift of questions. For this reason, I cannot tell you how to read or how to speak. I can only suggest an attitude. I can urge you to think about authority and relationship as you read and as you speak. I can ask you to savor the literal as well as the symbolic. I can ask you to read and to speak, to continue a relationship rather than to submit, dominate, or disrupt it. If you would read and speak as a woman, I recommend you take up your position as the absent object, claim your own difference rather than finding it in the claims of your brothers and fathers.

2

The Claim of Philia

Virginia Woolf said that women think back through their mothers.
This means several things. It means that the maternal connection
is always present in the daughters' lives. It means that we carry
our mothers around inside us in a way that our brothers do not
simply by virtue of our being women and our having first been
given to ourselves in a woman's gaze. For Virginia Woolf it means
that we have a lineage to be claimed, a lineage we can trace to an
event that occurred during the eighteenth century and one that,
were she writing history, we should take as having greater
significance than the Crusades or the Wars of the Roses:—women
began to write.[14]

But thinking back through our mothers, we may find our
inheritance burdensome, too. Fiction and poetry, social science
and philosophy, not to mention biology and chemistry are littered
with repudiations of our mothers, if not with their literal corpses.
Nineteenth century medical texts depicted women's bodies as
childlike, right down to the size of the brain cavity. Social science
teaches us that women are powerless and fearful. And all of this
knowledge comes to us as gender neutral. In poetry and film, in
theater and literature, that produced by men provides us with
mothers either fearsome or ethereal, either wholly sexed or wholly
desexed. To think back through our mothers may lead us to anger
at their powerlessness and ours.

Sometimes it seems, it must have seemed to those of us so
pleased to think more like men than women, that nothing good

could come of a maternal inheritance. A problem for the feminist teacher is to find a way of thinking back through our mothers, in the languages we have, in our institutional discourses without repudiating them, and by implication, ourselves. This is another dimension of the search for a woman's sentence.

I presented a version of this chapter in 1985 at the Conference on Curriculum Theory and Classroom Practice sponsored by the *Journal of Curriculum Theorizing*. Someone made a mistake in the program, so that rather than the title that heads this chapter, my presentation was entitled "The Claim of Philo." It was a marvelous mistake. It began the reclamation project which finally became this book. I first learned that my title had been modified when a colleague asked me, "Who is Philo?" I had then one of those moments when I suddenly understood what the presentation was about at a level that had been previously unavailable to me. It was then too that I understood the anger that deformed the work I describe in chapter 5, and it was then that I understood the importance of that anger. It was then that I understood this chapter to have emerged from a specifically female anger transformed into a pedagogy that asserts a gendered experience. That substitution of one letter for two was an uncannily economical summary of this entire book. My friend and colleague's question sent me back to a beginning I had nearly forgotten on my way to the claim of philia.

I might certainly have written "The Claim of Philo" at some time before "The Claim of Philia." Had I been reading David Hume rather than Ludwig Wittgenstein and Stanley Fish, I almost surely would have done so. Had I been inhabiting Hume's discursive universe, I would surely have been thinking then in terms of radical skepticism rather than of linguistic communities. I was persuaded by certain philosophers, social theorists, and literary critics that all knowing is a matter of perspective and commitment, and I learned to change the way that I thought about knowing, to change the way that I thought about thinking. Critical standards, norms, methodologies, procedures, the objects of knowledge themselves all became subjects of radical doubt, and the question of authority took on a particular urgency, as I think it must. This chapter is, in a way, a feminist teacher's response to radical doubt.

As a teacher I present authoritatively, authorized readings of authorized representations of things. My voice is the voice of tradition. But when the tradition is shown to be contingent, when the pleasingness of its dress and physiognomy is shown to be something like a matter of fashion, authority is arbitrary. As a graduate student I embraced the proposition that teaching is a rational act, the ends of which one achieves by drawing others into the rational conversations out of which is made the history of our culture. Then came Wittgenstein, Kuhn, Geertz, Nietzsche, Sartre, Lacan, Eagleton, Fish, Hartmann, Cavell, *et al.* to disturb my universe. If what we believe is what we cannot help believing, is, as they say, the world *tout court*, neither of our making nor independent of our making, what is the rational warrant for teaching? In what sense is teaching a rational act? The aesthetic resolutions which permit the literary critic to go on reading and judging, the philosopher to go on making claims about this and that, and the ethnographer to continue ethno-describing, did not seem to work for the teacher. I was talking about changing people's lives, their beings, I thought. A bad move in teaching is more serious than a stupid reading of *Othello* might be. What, after all, could count as a bad move and how would I recognize one when I made it? Having reached that point, however, I could get no further than the sedimented history of epistemology would take me. I knew that I wanted the world to be different, and I knew how. But I retained the faith in human reason that is the patrimony of our Enlightenment fathers.

That patrimony seemed a very small fortune indeed, quickly eaten up by taxes and other necessities. I decided to turn profligate and join the younger sons who had already determined to live it up until the money ran out. I followed them, Nietzsche and all the others, into the disreputable corners of antirationalism. I found uneasy refuge there. Within the terms of the epistemological dialectic—rational-antirational, I lodged uncomfortably. For to line up on one side or the other leaves me still too lonely and in my isolation possessed by the myth of a terrible power. Finding no asylum on either side, I dressed myself in the skeptic's style. A medallion impressed with a likeness of Hume's Philo could have hung around my neck. I fled to faith and probability. "I may be wrong," I said, "but I just know. Some things you just know. And you can be comfortable with those things and with acting on them if you act from love, from eros." Still, many before me have loved not wisely, but too well. In the economy of the rational, in kingdom of the rule of One, love in the wrong hands is a dangerous weapon. My teaching and work with colleagues has transformed my Enlightenment faith and agnosticism both, while keeping faith with both.

A different economy is needed, a register of language not assimilated to the rational so narrowly construed. For in the register of rationality, our brothers carry on their dialogue of difference and opposition. In this register is spoken the male relationship to language. In this register the son takes up his position. It is not a position the daughter can take. It should be understood when I talk about male and female, I am not talking about you or me. A woman may take the male position. In fact, to speak at all women have had often to stand just there in their brothers' places.

This chapter begins outside of that economy. It starts at a different place from which I moved to change the way, once again, that I thought about things. I began with a different question: Why does one feel a need to justify "authority?" Why do I? To answer that question, the methods of the detective served me better than those of the skeptic. I acknowledged the claim of Philo Vance and began an archaeology of the crime. I suspended my belief in the obvious, in what goes without saying. I found what goes without saying to be critical in my reconstruction. Let me lay out for you one fantasy of the scene of the crime:

> But perhaps, although the senses sometimes deceive us when it is a question of very small and distant things, still there are many other matters which one can certainly not doubt, although they are derived from the very same senses: that I am sitting here before the fireplace wearing my dressing gown, that I feel this sheet of paper in my hands, and so on. But how could one deny that these hands and that my whole body exist? Unless perhaps I should compare myself to insane people whose brains are so impaired by a stubborn vapor from a black bile that they continually insist that they are kings when they are in utter poverty, or that they are wearing purple robes when they are naked, or that they have a head made of clay, or that they are gourds, or that they are made of glass. But they are all demented, and I would appear no less demented if I were to take their conduct as a model for myself.
>
> All of this would be well and good, were I not a man who is accustomed to sleeping at night, and to undergoing in my sleep the very same things—or now and then even less likely ones—as do these insane people when they are awake.[15]

I am alone in my dressing gown. Of all of the congealed images of our collective cultural heritage, that one is the most horrifying. I am alone in my dressing gown, and you may be a cleverly constructed automaton sent here by an evil demon to deceive me. How can I trust you? Perhaps all of Western philosophy *is* a footnote to Plato, but surely Descartes' terror strikes to the heart of us all.[16] Perhaps our terror is even greater than his.

Without Descartes' perfect being, whose perfection entails, as a matter of logic—existence, and whose existence entails not only our own, but that of the material world and of other minds like ours, we may feel ourselves little better off than his lunatics. The cheerful American solution has been to negate the power of the image by invoking the charms of empiricism. "Don't worry none, them crazy dreams are only in your head."[17] Still, we sometimes find ourselves alone in our dressing gowns, without the ocular proof, unable to deny the ocular proof. Othello's problem. "I'll let you be in my dream if I can be in yours."[18]

Our common dream is a dream of language—a dream of a common language. One version of this dream has us engaged in struggle for mastery over language, what some call "the definition of reality," or more strongly, "the power to define reality." The ocular proof is disappeared right behind god. All we have is what we say, but ironically, words can't get us to the heart of this or any other matter. The word approximates nothing but itself, is mere inscription of desire on an ultimately illegible universe. Language, for some, becomes wholly self-referential. The question is, as Humpty Dumpty put it, "Who is to be master—that's all."

> "But 'glory' doesn't mean 'a knockdown dragout fight,' " said Alice. "When *I* use the word it does," replied Humpty Dumpty. "The question," said Alice, "is whether you can make a word mean anything you want it to."
> "The question is," said Humpty Dumpty, "Who is to be master—that's all."[19]

Such views of language interest us. Wittgenstein teaches us to ask who can take the position in which these are sensible views. He teaches us to ask to whom they can be meaningful. These questions lead to another clue in the scene we have been attempting to reconstruct.

During a faculty seminar on teaching the novel, a colleague in the English department remarked on the nineteenth-century female protagonist's trick of being the last to see that which should be most obvious, that which most concerns her. Emma Woodhouse is the last to know that Mr. Knightley must marry no one but herself, while the reader knows it very early in the book. Jane Eyre, that perspicacious and judicious reader of human affairs, takes forever to tumble to Rochester's regard for her. The protagonist's purblindness is not, however, the only common-place of the novel of female development at this time. The novel ends in one of two ways: either with the disgrace and death of the protagonist or with her courtship and actual or projected marriage. We know pretty early on in our reading which conclusion will be served. Nevertheless, having begun reading one of these novels we continue reading, through the time which should be spent preparing tomorrow's classes, past the time when we should have begun dinner preparations, well into time which should be given over to sleep and dreams. Perhaps they appeal to something we know, but have not yet acknowledged.

Perhaps this question of authority is not really an epistemo-logical problem. Or at least not merely an epistemological problem. Or not an epistemological problem within the commonly accepted purview of epistemology within which inferences are questions, but matters of trust are not.

The knowledge we suspect we have is dangerous knowledge in that it reveals the vulnerability that our epistemologies defend. And that vulnerability is not a female vulnerability. Perhaps by referring to that literary form which has been most congenial to women, and in which women's stories have been told most often we can get at our unacknowledged knowledge. Our subversive knowledge is not the knowledge that reason has its limits, but the knowledge that reason *sets* limits. It sets limits to our vulnerability. If the female *bildungsroman* can be read as a metaphor, if not a paradigm, of female education under patriarchy, we might possibly name that vulnerability.

The pilgrimage to identity and maturity for the female protagonist in the nineteenth-century novel takes her into dark places in which she discovers the male's guilty secret. From the moment of its discovery, she undertakes to claim and domesticate that secret. Her reward, her passage to personhood, is symbolized by her change of name. "Reader, I married him," begins the final chapter of *Jane Eyre*.

The outcome is not so felicitous for those women who refuse to acknowledge the claim of the male secret. Think of Catherine Earnshaw. However well married, Catherine Earnshaw never becomes for the reader Catherine Linton, although her daughter does for a time. But even she will become Earnshaw again at the novel's end. Heathcliff has no patronym to confer.

These novels may be read as stories of the daughter's seduction, but seduction with an interesting turn. The turn is that the seduction depends not on male but on female penetration. This is subversive. The text also takes the female reader to an odd place. Insofar as she identifies with the female protagonist, the female reader, she who knows what the protagonist does not, that which is most important to her, is in the very peculiar position of penetrating even as she is penetrated. She holds all of the clues. One secret is a danger to the protagonist. The secret of Rochester's mad wife is a danger to Jane Eyre. And yet we female readers align our interests with Rochester. We conspire with the male secret even as we participate in the struggle to discover, claim, and domestic it. That is the story of female education. It is the story of my education.

The secrets of these texts are also the secrets of our brothers' and fathers' interpretations of them. They put us in our place. Tony Tanner's imaginative and credible readings of *Jane Eyre* and *Wuthering Heights* are good examples of the way they do so. Most important to Tanner is the significance of Jane's telling her own story while Catherine's is a doubly-refracted tale. In Tanner's reading storytelling is a rite of passage. It is a ceremony in which the teller claims her name. "I am Jane Eyre. On such and such a day, such and such occurred, and started me on my journey to the present." This ritual formulation is the beginning of redemption, of the storyteller's abrogation of presocial passion to the claims of the sociable forms of language. Tanner locates the tragedy of *Wuthering Heights* in the wordlessness of Catherine and Heath-cliff's passion, in their determination to escape from "grammar." Catherine and Heathcliff deny the limits of human communion and so they fail to achieve personhood. They reject skepticism's knowledge—the knowledge of separation, the knowledge that we can never be totally comprehended by and can never totally comprehend the other.[20] I think of my education as, in fact, an education in the limits of human reason with all of the resonances that "limit" can carry.

Tanner's reading is heavy with epistemological anxiety. It is saturated with it. His reading is also an inevitable one. It works. It make sense. I have been persuaded by it. But whose reading is it? And what can it mean to the reader, the female reader, whose interests are aligned with both the protagonist and the seducer?

In Tanner's readings of the two texts, the romances are central. And yet, in *Jane Eyre* romance occupies a relatively small space in the novel. We do not meet Rochester until page 98; we leave him at page 281, not to meet him again until page 379 when we find him, significantly, crippled and blinded. Blind as Oedipus was blind. The story then winds down in some twenty pages concluding with the domestic arrangements of Diana and Mary and with St. John's impending death. Yet the romance remains the emotional center of the book—the romance and Rochester's guilty secret.[21]

Adrienne Rich reminds us, though, of the substantial time that Jane spends in the company of other women, some of whom teach and nurture her, all of whom provide her with examples, good and bad, for leading her life.[22]

Sandra Gilbert and Susan Gubar recall us to the significance of Jane's anger in her story, in particular her anger about woman's lot:

Who blames me? Many no doubt; and I shall be called discontented. I could not help it: the restlessness was in my nature; it agitated me to pain sometimes. Then my sole relief was to walk along the corridor of the third story, backwards and forwards, safe in the silence and solitude of the spot and allow my mind's eye to dwell on whatever bright visions rose before it—and certainly they were many and glowing; . . . [but] it is vain to say human beings ought to be satisfied with tranquility; they must have action; and they will make it if they cannot find it. . . . Women are supposed to be very calm generally; but women feel just as men feel; they need exercise for their efforts as much as their brothers do; they suffer from too rigid a restraint, too absolute a stagnation, precisely as men suffer; and it is narrow-minded in their more privileged fellow-creatures to say that they ought to confine themselves to making puddings and knitting bags. It is thoughtless to condemn them, or laugh at them, if they seek to do more or learn more than custom has pronounced necessary for their sex.[23]

This outburst occurs just two pages prior to Jane's first meeting with Rochester and is interrupted by the "slow Ha! Ha!" of Bertha's keeper. Gilbert and Gubar argue that while Bertha is literally the madwoman in Rochester's attic, she is also figuratively the madwoman in Jane's. They note that Bertha appears and acts only following occasions on which Jane has repressed anger and resentment. Bertha's attempt to burn Rochester in his bed is Jane's doing. Claiming and domesticating Rochester's guilty secret requires Jane to tame her own guilty anger. Jane Ire.[24]

If Jane's angry outbursts are read as replacing the romance as the novel's emotional center, and if we observe that its female characters are either incompetent or the keepers of other women, surrogates for absent men, it is clear that the skeptical Tanner reading is a partial one. A different focus can yield a subtext which contests the story we have assumed. This is part of what we mean when we talk about reading as a woman. Traditional readings of this novel spell an affirmative encoding of nineteenth-century gender relations, as do traditional readings of *Wuthering Heights.* So do such postmodern readings as Tanner's. But if we shift our focus, those same gender relations become a critical target. And finally they express a peculiarly female relationship to language. In Homans' schema,[25] the doubling strategies of *Jane Eyre's* narrative are examples of a female strategy of reclaiming the figure, of literalizing and embodying the abstract.

Still, partial as it is, Tanner's reading compels our attention. So compelling is that reading that it blinds us to what is most obvious. We readers collude in the male's guilty secret, and our collusion blinds us to the significance of that secret to our own lives. The secret is a sexual one. Rochester is all brooding male sexuality. He has a mad wife in his attic and a bastard daughter in his drawing room. Twenty years Jane's senior, he will initiate her, a fatherless motherless daughter, into the mysteries of adult sexuality. In return, Jane will expiate his guilt by vanquishing both his madwoman and her own. The contract will be sealed by her taking his name, the Name-of-the-Father. In becoming Jane Rochester, Jane Eyre authorizes Rochester's reproductive authority; in doing so she legitimates him. He will become the authorized author of her children, and the center of her authorized autobiography. All will be made legible within the code of patriarchal authority. Adele Varennes, also Rochester's daughter, has only her mother's name, the faithless Celine. He

who violated the code of patriarchy in his relations with Celine
has been brought back to it. He is now its legitimate representative. Rochester's secret has a double aspect: the other face of the
secret of wide sexual experience is the male's knowledge that
paternity is always ambiguous. Outside the bonds of patriarchy all
women may be faithless. Think how much of literature involves
mistaken paternity—the finding of lost fathers and lost children,
the reclamation of patrimony.

Feminist psychoanalysts and literary theorists understand the
ambiguity of paternity to be the impulse to and foundation of
patriarchal domination. Patriarchal domination is written in the
register of the symbol, the totalizing discursive practices congealed around the Name-of-the-Father. Jane Gallop writes:

> The authorized partakes of the legal and the name. The authorized
> legitimate thought bears the author's name; the unauthorized, the
> illegitimate lacks the Name-of-the-Father. The Name-of-the-Father,
> let us here signal, is a powerful Lacanian term, actually a Lacanian
> displacement of . . . the Oedipal Father, absolute primal father.
> Whereas Freud's Oedipal Father might be taken for a real biological
> father, Lacan's Name-of-the-Father operates explicitly in the register
> of language. The Name-of-the-Father is the fact of the attribution of
> paternity by Law, by language. Paternity cannot be perceived,
> proven, known with certainty; it must be instituted by the
> judgment of the mother's word.[26]

The mother's "Yes," as she offers her body as a charm against
anxiety, places her in the register of the symbol. She is
disembodied. The universe is legible. Psychoanalytic feminist
theory, taken together with the variety of constructivist and
critical views of knowledge, all, in one way or another,
problematize Descartes' *cogito*. His disembodied "I," though,
continues to insist, as Virginia Woolf put it, "A shadow lying
across the page, hiding the landscape behind it."[27] The tones of its
insistence are saturated with the father's project—to wrest the
child from ambiguity and subjectivity. The father's "I," given in
the mother's "yes" sets the stage for patriarchy. It becomes also
the pre-text for the epistemology of skepticism.

The invocation of the Name-of-the-Father also secures to the
fathers political and economic power. Since Engels' study of the
origins of the state and family many scholars have linked family

arrangements and the control of reproduction through custom and state legislation to the imperatives of private property. The holders of property have an interest in controlling the succession and distribution of that property. Since it is impossible to fix paternity with certainty and since historically the holders of property have been predominantly male, a set of rules and procedures evolved which operated to limit the extent of doubt. The authorized discursive practices figured in the Name-of-the-Father enable the inference of paternity. The control of female sexuality through the formal rules of distribution and succession are the social, political, and economic equivalents to the methodological rules that minimize uncertainty, the threat of epistemological anxiety, in the natural and social sciences. The strategies of doubt, of probability, and of inference operate with respect to natural and social objects just as those strategies operate in the realm of property distribution.

When we associate sexuality and property we begin to comprehend the extent to which production and reproduction are all mixed up together and to see just what is at stake for patriarchy.

It scarcely needs saying at this point that education both produces and reproduces culture, nor that education therefore reproduces property and power relations. Let us follow Grumet's suggestion, then, and take the word "reproduction" to its roots:

> If our understanding of education rests on our understanding of the reproduction of society, then the reproduction of society itself rests upon our understanding of reproduction as a project that shapes our lives, dominating our sexual, familial, economic, political, and finally, educational experience.[28]

Grumet unravels the several intentions expressed in the phrase "reproducing ourselves." First there is the literally intended meaning of biological reproduction, not what we are about in schools. Second comes the metaphorical expression—"cultural reproduction." Finally, insofar as we are self-reflective and self-conscious, the notion of reproducing ourselves contains a critical content. The critical significance of the expression is the concern of the curriculum, which, as Grumet says, "becomes our way of contradicting biology and ideology."[29] Or at least it ought to. Contradicting biology, argues Grumet, is the paternal project of the curriculum:

[To contradict] the inferential nature of paternity, the paternal project of the curriculum, is to claim the child, to teach him or her to master the language, the rules, the games and the names of the fathers.[30]

The problem as I see it is how to honor the claims, the interest of the paternal project, without, again borrowing from Grumet, "becoming traitors to our sex." We may read the feminist educator's project then as contradicting the patriarchal claims of culture while honoring the paternal interest.

Grumet agues that too many of us mistake the interest of the paternal project in claiming the child as demanding denial of the maternal claim, of the feminine. Her conception of contradiction requires us to deny neither. Shall we say that the curriculum project intends to give the child to himself or to herself? Or at least that it ought to? How is this possible if our discursive practices are the totalizing, legitimizing practices of patriarchal authority that they seem to be? We are our fathers' daughters and sons, the "I" that casts its shadow across the page.

The curriculum is, our practices within curriculum are, discursive practices. We are not mute in the classroom. To borrow from the code of production, language is our medium of exchange. And our talk is about texts, authorized texts—cultural productions. We can talk about nondiscursive practices and modes of knowing, but even these are heavy with patriarchal authority. The gaze itself is a speculum of patriarchy. Feminist film theorists, for example, argue that a feminist film may be an impossible notion. They wonder whether a woman filmmaker can accomplish anything beyond simply shifting the relations of dominance and submission within the visual codes of patriarchy. Ways of looking as well as ways of talking are conventional and constitutive. The specular women of patriarchy are mirrors of patriarchal desire in which the image of Woman is constructed. The relationship between Woman and the image of the specular women who must find themselves there recapitulates, in perverse fashion, the imaginary relationship to the maternal. The gaze of the one who nourishes is appropriated by the one who dominates. The question in all of the arts, and in education, is whether the power of the artist and the power of the teacher necessarily place her in the masculine position. Grumet, once more, states the problem succinctly for the teacher:

Teachers and students manipulate signs and symbols. The medium through which they communicate is knowledge, the codes and methods of the academic disciplines by now highly abstracted from the material necessity and politics that originally shaped them.[31]

Still, as she says, the look dominates the classroom, and it is the look of the scopophiliac, the one who sees but is not seen. It is the look of patriarchy which:

> . . . Rather than finding a language to name and appropriate the interests and history that have named him, the student too often sees the perspective behind the look as impersonal, inevitable and determining. Lifted from history, motives and politics, the look of the teacher is endorsed with an authority that disclaims history, motives and politics.[32]

It is, she says, not easy to be a teacher in today's schools. We are our fathers' daughters. In feeling the weight of this knowledge, I understand that the crucial question for me is not authority *qua* authority, but women's authority—a room of our own.

We women who have taken seriously the claim that legitimate authority must be legitimized have discovered the father's secret and taken it for our own. "Reader, I married him." But the female professor is a strange creature—neither father nor mother. Often she is merely a surrogate for absent fathers, reproducing their order, asserting patriarchal authority over the mistresses of misrule. For a feminist professor teaching women's studies courses the role is not altogether a comfortable one. She begins to understand that she authorizes that which keeps us all in thrall. She has said "yes," to the patriarchal imperative. Her difficulty is most keenly felt when she teaches female students, many of whom will insist that she be a good mom—a position that often seems the only alternative to the surrogate patriarch. But the discursive practices through which the paternal project is expressed need not deny the feminist project. The paternal project is not necessarily a patriarchal project. For female teachers the possibility of dialogue within the discursive practices of the fathers is possible only if we can describe a woman's sentence.

We need a voice of our own. As Grumet says, we need to reclaim the gaze, "seeing others and being seen without being reduced to our images."[33]

Let us fantasize the Cartesian original situation in a different voice; let us see it with different eyes. Let us resymbolize it by reinstituting the literal embodied world:

It is Sunday, September 15, 2:00 p.m. I am alone in the house. I am sitting in my study at the back of the house looking out over the road that dips and curves and rises and dips and curves and rises again until it falls away from sight completely. We live in the country. We have no near neighbors; the nearest cows even are half a mile away. Sometimes on my way home from work I have to wait for them to cross the road to their barn for milking. I have learned something interesting about herds of cows: once they have started to cross the road they cannot be stopped. It takes our neighbor's cows about ten minutes. At the end of the line comes the boy on his motorbike. We smile and wave. I don't mind waiting. I enjoy the cows in their single-minded concentration. Usually, though, I see no one. I see no one now. There are no cows, no friendly boys on motorbikes. The silence is interrupted only by the angry whining of the hornets in the eaves and the complaining of my word processor: "Hurry up, hurry up," it hums.

It's a rare autumn day in central New York, not a hint of rain or mist or cold. I am barefoot. The window is open. The trees across the valley are just turned. There are books and notebooks on the floor, piled in a semicircle around my desk. Some are heaped on my easy chair and more are stacked on the table. I am working, trying to find my way through this chapter. I am also listening for the oven timer. There are two loaves of graham flour bread in the oven. We bring sandwiches to our offices during the week. Sometimes I check the road to see if the cats need to be chased back to the safe boundaries of our property.

The gray cat and the orange one. Out of the corner of my eye I watch to see that the puppy doesn't eat another corner of *The Philosophical Investigations* or squat on the completed pages of this book on the floor beside my chair. At 5:00 I will cover this machine and bring the vegetables for dinner in from the garden. I will scrub them and chop them up—small carrots, leeks, tomatoes, and parsley for stew. Then I will mix the batter for biscuits and set various things to simmer on the stove. We will sit down with our drinks, the pets in for the night, to watch the news and talk about this and that, maybe about this book, maybe just gossip. . . .

Production and reproduction get mixed up together. This account does not make me uneasy. It does not occur to me that the writer might not be alone in her house, that perhaps lurking behind the door or waiting in the basement. . . . This version of "alone in my dressing gown" roots the speaker, her thought and her work in the places and stuff of life among living creatures. There is another important difference between this account and the Cartesian fantasy, and that is to be found in the language and the different projections of power behind the different languages. Both are expressions of vulnerability.

Descartes' vulnerability is thrust on him; mine is chosen. Descartes' vulnerability separates him from the world; mine connects me. To be vulnerable for Descartes is to be impoverished or naked or made of glass. Those who are vulnerable are demented, but Descartes is not. Still he sometimes sleeps and dreams. His account is a dream of vulnerability repressed in unconscious, but returning to haunt him in the figures of madness.

I am alone in the house, and I too am thinking. But my version of thinking takes place, literally, in a world of cats and puppies and husbands and vegetables and oven timers. My version claims the world and acknowledges the world's claim on me. My claim is the claim of philia.

> Claim: territory, enclosure, affirm, plead, requirement, require, demand, request, possess, estate, appropriate, desire, right, have a right, litigation. Litigation? My claim is disputed? It must be proved.
> Proof: invulnerable, resisting, impassive. Dry, hard, unfeeling. My claim is my territory. My territory is invulnerable. I enclose myself in my claim and am proof against attack. All philosophy, said Nietzsche, is a desire of the heart filtered and made abstract. The question is—who is to be master, that's all.
> Philia: not eros, not agape, certainly not logos. Loving, friendly, love of friends or of one's fellow man—social sympathy. A virtue Aristotle denied to women. The question is—who are our friends?

The "claim of philia" is an oxymoron, or if you prefer, a contradiction. "Love of one's companion creatures" contradicts most of the synonyms Roget gives us for "claim." Acknowledging the claim of philia, that philia is or has or makes a claim creates a new thing—a thing in which production and reproduction are mixed up together. To be affiliated, to acknowledge the requirements of affiliation, the demands that we make on each other for affiliation, is to temper our need for proof, to make tolerable the ambiguity of paternity, and the child's loss of the mother. To acknowledge philia as a claim is to acknowledge ourselves as public persons whose private selves we express in our language games.

In the nineteenth century female *bildungsroman*, philia is exiled from the language game of claiming, although it is often the subtext of that game. Contradiction hurts. Jane Eyre's autobiography is her final production as she retreats into the private and subjective world of the family. Jane Eyre, lighter than air, heir to nothing,[34] marries him and repudiates in that act the Jane who paced the battlements of Thornfield, raging for power and freedom, gaining only a new servitude. In asserting and confirming the Name-of-the-Father, Jane affirms Lacan's claim that identity is impossible for women. So does Catherine Earnshaw, whose insistence on claiming the literalness of nature and speaking the mother tongue requires her death.[35]

The problem of authority is rooted in the inferential nature of paternity. But authority is also a problem for women. I am Jane Eyre. As good students, we female academics mastered the fathers' language games, asserting their claims as our own, taking their names and titles as our own. Until Virginia Woolf introduced her to us, we never gave a thought to Shakespeare's sister Judith,[36] although our Marxist brothers taught us to weep for all the mute inglorious Miltons.

We learned to suppress and overcome our incomprehension of certain texts. We learned to stop asking impertinent questions. We learned what was irrelevant, philosophically uninteresting, and of minor artistic interest. We learned to live with our guilt over the suspicion that we were all of those things. Usually we repressed our rage at institutions and arrangements which were not made for us, happy to have an equal chance. We repressed our rage allowing it to return to ourselves and sisters. I think of my own female students entering a newly coeducational institution. Facilities for females are simply other-named versions of male arrangements. Fraternities and sororities. Red Raiders and Lady Raiders. Men and women side by side in classrooms, living through the fathers' curriculum. They are our daughters; they are our fathers' daughters. And no more than we did, do they express rage against those who silence them in classrooms. When Bertha ventures out from our attics, the attics of those of us who play the fathers' claim game, it is only to engage in a knockdown, dragout scholarly attack. Glory.

We transformed the madwoman's claim into the claim of reason. In doing so we made the madwoman's anger an abstraction. A central part of the feminist educative project has been to reclaim and own our anger, to comfort Bertha, to sit her before the fire in the living room. We feel a tension, though, between our anger and the claim of patriarchal authority. If one is beside oneself with anger, or with any other emotion, one is not thinking reasonably, therefore authoritatively, with and of the curriculum.

Women students' and teachers' anger comes form their sense of being always wrong, always other. As Mary Wollstonecraft said, "It is the consciousness of always being female which degrades our sex."[37] Our repression of our anger is a denial of that consciousness. We have given over wholly to the claims of the fathers in order to find ourselves places in the codes of production. For Virginia Woolf, denial of our anger was essential; anger hobbles women's work. Her criticism of *Jane Eyre* is leveled at Bronte's anger. However understandable Bertha's madness, all our safety requires that she be kept in the attic.

Beyond Woolf's horizon lies the contemporary feminist view most often concerned with "empowering pedagogies," the love that follows anger. Those who look in this direction assert that the educational project in general should empower persons, all persons, to live their lives with integrity, with honesty, and in freedom to develop their full human capacities: capacities for creation, production, affiliation, and nurturance. Beginning from this point much feminist writing about curriculum and teaching addresses itself to a felt imperative of developing nonhierarchical, nonauthoritarian ways of teaching. This imperative leads us straight back to the patriarchal formulation of authority and results for some, Susan Stanford Friedman for example, in the suspicion that authority in a feminist classroom is a contradiction.[38] One can either speak the Name-of-the-Father or fall silent. This opposition is, of course, a construction within the bipolar logic of logocentric thought. While an interest in developing nonpatriarchal curricular and pedagogical forms is desirable, it is undesirable that the project be conceived within the limits of this logic.

We are women who certify male knowledge, who confer the names of the fathers. We are women who work through the power of the totalizing discourses through which we enter the cultural conversation. In this, we contradict our biology. We must acknowledge that. If we deny that our power proceeds from our appropriation of the symbolic, we are disingenuous. We are our fathers' daughters. We can either stop there, secure in our positions as father surrogates, we can be good girls, or we can aim truly for power, the power which must be taken, cannot be conferred, by understanding and celebrating the contradictions in our own lives. Analyzing these contradictions will take us to a second stage—contradicting patriarchal culture.

The central contradiction in the female intellectual's life is that as women who operate in the symbolic register, we often encounter ourselves as Other to ourselves. We identify with Jane Eyre at the same time that we read from the masculine position. We participate in the male guilty secret. Our participation need not be collusion, however. Though speaking within the totalizing discourses of the symbolic, we can continue to assert connection with the literal and imaginary, with the image that receives the text, the pre-Oedipal, pregrammatical, imaginary. Our simultaneous connection with the literal and the symbolic is our privilege. The question of paternal authority is my problem only insofar as I choose to share my life with the fathers and brothers. We become though, the good girls, so identified with the fathers' power, that if we don't marry them we join our brothers in trying to kill them off. Freud was mistaken when he said that we must take sides and that the father's is the infinitely better side.

To take a feminine position and claim the presymbolic literal as the subtext of our work is not to celebrate the amorphous, thoroughly individualized, subjective, male-romanticized, theatricalized version of the feminine. Rousseau did a bad thing. Shakespeare knew better. It is not necessary that we bake cookies for our seminars, spend our lives at potluck dinners, or dress ourselves in the flowing robes and recondite truths of the Sibyl, in order to resist the claims of patriarchy. The Eternal Feminine is a patriarchal image saturated with the guilt, uncertainty, and sentimentality of patriarchy.

The conflict between nurturance and authority is symbolic. If we assert the value of mom's world over dad's, we enter the nexus of symbolic exchange. We become sexless, ironically at the very moment when we assert our sex. As ourselves and as Other to ourselves we must see each as giving point to the other to engender a new thing and a gendered thing. Conversation between the symbolic and the literal or imaginary discloses a world of alternative practice in which the conversation counts more than the assertion.

While patriarchal forms of knowledge and discursive practices are authoritarian, do forbid conversation, they are not authoritative. Indeed, if the psychoanalytic view has anything to it, the authoritarian posture is a substitute for authority. Focusing on production and exchange, patriarchy represses knowledge of the importance of reproduction, the realm of its anxiety. But what is repressed always returns.

Authority emerges as a problem only when one restricts one's understanding of human relations to the realm of production. The literal facts of reproducing life, bearing and raising children, growing and cooking food, making art, etc. give us back to ourselves and to each other. It is not a question of biological sex. I am alone in the house. But for me the world does not recede. It does not dip below some horizon, some illusion of the untruthful eye. It cannot recede. Quite the contrary. The world is given point by my solitude. For even as I sit alone in my room, I feel a pull on my attention that necessarily attaches me to the world. Our intellectual work ought to give point to and signify those attachments. Our attachments ought to give point to that work. This is the claim of philia. The woman's sentence will be instinct with the claim of philia.

Philia defies abstraction. One can be affiliated only with particular others. Women, for both biological and cultural reasons, remain connected to the particular in ways that men do not. A woman remains connected to the maternal body, literalizes the maternal body in her femaleness. But philia also defies individualistic, privatized subjectivity. The claim of philia is a claim on both men and women. The claim of patriarchy and its single-sided concern with certainty and totalizing discourses, its mistake regarding the nature and source of authority in the interest of repressing patriarchal anxiety and toward the end of turning from the primal love for the mother, transforms knowledge into a product lodged in the system of free-market exchange. Romanticized, ritualized, sentimentalized, theatricalized, privatized claims of matriarchy similarly wedge knowledge into the cramped corners of commodity relations. My knowledge, not yours. The

claim of philia turns us to genuine alternative practice, practice in
which knowledge is a use value. It binds us together in common
work.

The claim of philia turns us to the text—the product—and the
texture of our reading both. The trick is to appropriate the text and
to let it continue to be itself—to be near yet separate. We can do
that if we recollect the textures of our readings, if we appreciate
the textures of others' readings. These readings will be unauthorized texts, and these are the basis, but not the sum, of our
authority as readers and speakers. Our readings, our affiliation
with the totalizing discourses of our texts even as we link them to
the image, the imaginary real, the literal replaced by its figures, is
the source of authority and power. Every book is the secret. Every
secret has a subtext which betrays the secret. Text and subtext
come together in conversation to create a new thing.

One of my most vivid memories is of the day I learned to, or
rather of the day I began to, read. It was the summer before I
entered kindergarten. I was in the hospital recovering from an
emergency appendectomy. My mother had undergone one three
weeks previously, and the family joke was that I had to do
whatever my mother did. I was four years old. In the hospital at
the same time was an eight-year-old girl. She had also had an
appendectomy. She was fully recovered by the time I met her, but
she was not permitted to go home until her mother raised the
money for the hospital bill. While she was waiting for her mother,
Cathy came regularly to my room to read to me. I liked being read
to; no one had ever read to me before. When I was able to leave
my bed, we used to walk down the hall to where Cathy slept. I
remember that a mattress had been laid down for her on the floor
beneath a window at the end of the corridor. Her poverty
disentitled her to a room. We snuggled down in Cathy's little nest
then, and she read my favorite book to me over and over again.
We were never bored. It was a little golden book with a bright
green cover. On the cover, two kids, a boy and a girl, were
wearing yellow slickers and splashing in puddles. My favorite part
of the story was the splashing and the singing of "Hayfoot,
strawfoot." I was told recently what that means, but I've forgotten
it again. Something to do with some war I think. All of a sudden,
one day, I could read my book all by myself. All of a sudden, I
knew, really understood, the way letters made words and words

made sentences. I could read that book, and I could read any other book too. I never wanted to do anything but read after that.

My great pleasure is coming home from the library or bookstore with an armload of new books. I love the moment of decision: Which shall I read first? When I was a little girl, I dawdled on my way home from the library, thinking over my selections, thinking about the books I had had to leave behind because I could not carry them. I loved the anticipation as much as the reading. Now I drive. When I get home, I prolong the ritual of making tea, settling into my corner with my cigarettes, a pen, a new pad, my dog, a cat if I can get one to come. I turn each book over several times, reading the book jackets, checking indices of the nonfiction ones, delaying the moment of commitment, enjoying the prospect of commitment. All of my texts retain for me the textures of my days of approach, the moment of anticipation and surprise. All of them are shot through with the immediate uses to which I put them in constructing my own life. These are illegitimate uses, some would say.

These are unauthorized parts of the readings, not nonreadings, but readings that the author, the authorized reader, could not have anticipated. My acknowledging and embracing the unauthorized parts of my readings and of those of others is my acknowledgment of the claim of philia and the source of my authority as a teacher. The trick is to let the unauthorized inform the authorized without distorting it. This is the root sense, the radical sense of information—to form, to shape. Authority is conferred by our willingness to claim the shapes we make and to lend our bodies for awhile to conform to the shapes around us. Our teaching and our authority become transparent in the face of the claim of philia, a claim that demands that we let our language speak us even as we speak it.

If there is a feminist revolution that strikes deeper than affirmative action curricula, and I think there is, it is a revolution of the body. It is the revolution of the peasant who knows that one cannot eat ideas and still have the strength to carry the world. It is a revolution in which doubleness is welcomed; it is a conversation rather than a debate, a question rather than an assertion.

3

The Nature and Sources of
Teacher Authority

Between student teachers and their supervisors, a greater intimacy
than that found in any other student-teacher relationship
inevitably develops. In a way the relationship is almost familial. It
resembles that of colleagues who team teach together. We may not
even like each other, but we have certain responsibilities and cares
together that devolve on our knowledge of each other's
vulnerability. A teacher is exposed even if she tries to hide. Her
failures are as open as her successes. Everything she does is open
to judgment—her speech and gestures, her dress, her makeup,
her hair, her intelligence, her poise, even her sense of humor. Like
members of a family, those of us who work together in classrooms
know the worst. We become, as family members do, protective of
each other. It is probably not insignificant that we share the same
children.

During the semesters that I work with student teachers, I am
rarely alone. Whenever I reach my office from home or class or
lunch, someone is there ahead of me asking for advice, for
reassurance, sometimes just talk. If I stay away from my office, my
home telephone rings continually. The student-teaching experience makes a person fragile. Everything seems bound up with
success. Success seems impossible. Student teachers are alter-
nately frightened and eager. The semester is a time when many of
them find themselves interrogating the basis of their own lives,

their commitments, their relationships with others, the justifiabil-
ity of all of their actions. They begin poking into motivations,
prodding the dark corners of their psyches. They become sensitive
to the enormity of teaching—to its ethical and political ramifica-
tions. That may be, of course, because my student teachers have
never before had much to do with people outside of their own
highly privileged social and economic class. This first experience
has the effect of a shock.

I find myself in parked cars at midnight, hours after the end of
the seminar meeting, on the telephone at 7:00 a.m. advising,
encouraging, and conferring with student teachers in crisis. The
suspicion of the impossibility of their being good enough, both
skillful enough and moral enough, strikes over and over again,
semester after semester. I'm no longer embarrassed by students
weeping in my office. Tears are always close to the surface.
Everything is close to the surface.

I was talking once with another person in my department who
works with student teachers. I was complaining about the
demands on my emotional energy, about what sometimes seemed
an excessive dependency on the part of my students. I said
something like, "What is it about this work that makes otherwise
self-confident and successful young men and women fall apart?
Even those who really are doing quite well in the classroom are
plagued all day long by the things that go bump in the night." He
was amused. He said that he had never seen anyone fall apart. He
suggested that I elicit that response. I'm quite certain now that he
was right. My students were learning more from me than I knew.

Since the days of my own high school teaching, I had been
certain that questions of method and technique were embedded in
complex moral, political, and psychological considerations. That is
the way that I teach my methods seminars. My students, then,
when they enter their public school classrooms are particularly
sensitive to the moral problematics of teaching. In my own career
as a high school teacher, I had been troubled by questions of
power and authority. I suspect that a female intellectual of
working class background is among those most likely to be
troubled by such questions. We know how radically one can be
changed by one's education. And I knew that I meant for
education to change both persons and the world. These questions
were greatly complicated for me by the habit of distrust gained
from my education in philosophy and social theory. My

theorizing, then, and consequently, that of my students remained embedded in the traditions of philosophical idealism toward which I had always been drawn as a student. It is clear to me now that I taught my students to be as uncertain of their legitimacy as I was of my own.

I wrote the first version of this chapter in 1982. It was the beginning of my second year as a university teacher. It was only the second time I had ever worked with student teachers. It was then that I began to think about the peculiar vulnerability of teaching, both my own and that of others. I did not realize then, however, that I was talking about my own vulnerability. As I try now to gather up the threads of this work and weave them into this text, I see just how loudly insistent our histories are and how persistent the themes that define those histories. Six years ago I thought I was working through the unique relationship to power, authority, and language of a particularly situated group of beginning teachers. Reading *their* words now, I hear my own voice too.

The initial work that went into this essay marks a first approach to the discursive shift which is one of the themes of this book. My first inclination in thinking about authority was to appeal to the experts. (I had always been a good student. I once told a high school student of mine that the difference between a teacher and a student is that the teacher knows where to look things up.) However, I did not recognize then my anger with the experts. Nor did anyone who read the initial version of the essay notice it. There is absolutely no good reason for me to be talking to or about Gilbert Ryle. Yet the conversation is quite lengthy. How could I have failed to notice, and why do I repeat an irrelevant conversation here? It is only apparently irrelevant. Its subtext is everything that this book is about. To demonstrate what I mean I have left the conversation with Ryle exactly as it was written in 1982, including the pervasive generic "he" even when I refer to myself or to all of us. In the remainder of the chapter, I move back and forth between my present and my 1982 readings to call your attention to the patterns of the work as I trace them now and to follow the trajectory of a feminist discursive shift in conversation with tradition.

This essay was written initially a short time after I completed my Ph.D. At the University of Rochester at that time, the Ph.D. in Education was an interdisciplinary degree. What that meant was that candidates for the degree were required to study with other faculty in other departments. I spent a good deal of time in the philosophy department. There, we students learned, philosophy is something one does. It is not something one studies. One professor pronounced in such a way as to leave no doubt, the irrelevance of historical philosophy to the enterprise. In order to *do philosophy* in this environment, one had to learn to talk back to the likes of Gilbert Ryle. In the field of education, at the same time, Ryle seemed nearly an obligatory item in any bibliography. Even Maxine Greene, whom one might suspect of having little use for such philosophy, was to invoke him numerous times. But there is something even more important. Just as our brothers must, so must we daughters talk back to our fathers. And we have only their language and traditions to do it in. The terms of the discussion are already laid out; we can either speak or be silent.

I do not mean to diminish the importance of Ryle's work to either philosophy or education. Its status as a major achievement is well deserved. But it is the wrong language for talking about the things I want to talk about, and my frustration and anger hum along beneath the entire conversation not loud but distracting. The language conceals that frustration. The trick, to borrow from another philosopher, is to discover how to do other things with words.

In *The Concept of Mind* Gilbert Ryle introduced two distinctions which became commonplace in discussions of curriculum and teaching. These are the distinctions between *knowing how* and *knowing that*; and *achievement*, or occurrent, words and *task* or dispositional words. In making the first distinction Ryle was concerned to abolish the "intellectualist" doctrine that knowing is the apprehension of truth. Instead, he argued that we quite sensibly use 'know' when we refer to a person's learned capacity for and tendency to engage in certain kinds of performances, and that these performances are no different in kind from 'mental' performances. The second distinction makes the point that words having to do with cognition can be categorized as either achievement words or task words. In the cognitive domain, "achievement" and "task" do not pick out two different kinds of things. Achievement words, words such as "solve," "know," "find," "see," etc. are episodic and descriptive of temporally isolated occurrences; task words, words such as "puzzling," "learning," "searching," and "looking," are dispositional and imply that the actor has acquired certain tendencies which are aroused or activated in appropriate circumstances. Achievement words denote the successful outcomes of tasks.[39]

The means-end rationality which dominates both curriculum and teaching is well-served by these distinctions; however, the means-end rationality itself is too limiting to any discussion of teaching. As an achievement word, "teaching" has a restrictive utility. Simply as a matter of logic, teaching, regarded as an achievement, can be said to have occurred only in circumstances in which it is deemed successful. Clearly such restrictiveness violates ordinary understanding. In fact, we talk about teaching in all sorts of contexts in which the learning hoped for fails to materialize. Ineffective teaching is still teaching. It would be nonsense for me to say of something I did in the classroom last week on observing the results of today's examination, "I thought I was teaching, but I was mistaken."

Ryle's distinction permits us to try to isolate the activities, the tasks, implied by the successful outcome of teaching. In Ryle's account as it is understood by educators, the dispositional definition of teaching becomes the "heedful" application of acquired skills in order to achieve some specified educational purpose. A teacher is one who employs the skills appropriate to achieving a particular end, *i.e.* the student's learning X.

The word "task" applied to teaching, and indeed, the means-end rationality in which it is embedded, is misleading. Its use has critical consequences for our thinking about education. A task is typically imposed from without; it is not merely necessary but also desirable that tasks be prosecuted in a routinized unselfconscious fashion. A task, moreover, signifies an obligation which, if not unpleasant, provokes minimal personal engagement. If teaching is a task, it is a very peculiar sort of task.

Teaching is not simply (or perhaps even simply not) a question of technique employed in the prosecution of some task. Teaching *is* dispositional, but that disposition is or should be something more than a goal-directed response tendency, something more that "knowing what to do in order to _____." Any discussion of teaching should comprehend the teacher's warrant and authority for teaching what he or she teaches.

Ryle's picture of teaching is drawn along a straight line that cuts through the nonsense and mess of mind and consciousness; A teaches X to B. What could be cleaner? What could be more elegant in its simplicity? The relationship is said to be triadic. Such linear perspective suggests that once X has been identified and the logical means for transferring X from A to B determined, there is nothing more to be said. The problem even from within that perspective, though, is, as Scheffler observed, that the achievement-task distinction enables us only to *exclude* certain activities from the "task" definition of teaching. Regarding the matter of what we *ought* to include, we are clueless.[40] As soon as we raise questions regarding what we ought to do, problems of trust and distrust sneak in, and the curtain is raised on the difficulty that the play of mind and consciousness cause us; the opacity of mind taunts us. I shall explore the implications of trust and distrust, and the opacity of other minds specifically in chapter 4.

Ryle's formulation is a marvelous example of the totalizing tendencies of patriarchal rhetoric. He is concerned to offer rules of exclusion, rules according to which things might be called by their proper names. He is concerned with assimilating and analogizing all teaching experience and to sorting its terms into relatively simple sets of oppositions. The assumption here is that if we can say clearly what we mean, we shall be able to do cleanly what we intend. The mess of everyday life, the clang of bells, the intercom interrupting a lively classroom discussion, Robby tipping his chair over backwards, the child who comes to school unfed—when we "say what we mean" we surrender these and their claim on us.

Many writers have argued that a linear model of teaching and learning is inadequate. Neil Hertz claimed to demonstrate that the apparent series in the triadic relationship is in fact a proportion. The usual triadic formulation, some version of A teaches X to B, Hertz says, does not express the pedagogical relationship. He argued instead for a relationship in which the text stands between teacher and student as the world comes to stand between mother and child. Just as the child must cathect to the world, the student shifts his cathexis to the text. The teacher is to his discipline, to particular authors and texts, as the student is to the teacher.[41] What happens when we multiply out the proportion? We are left with the student's relationship to the discipline. Does that mean that in the successful outcome of teaching the teacher has simply disappeared, been canceled out like the mother in Lacan's story of language? In a sense yes, but not exactly. The teacher remains present to the student through the text which now mediates the pedagogical attachment.

Wittgenstein taught us to think about knowledge acquisition as a process of initiation into various language games and of learning as mastering the techniques of those language games. A person who has mastered a technique knows simultaneously how-and-that. To know anything at all is to know how to do something. What the master knows is how to participate in experience in such a way as to create new facts. Initiation into a language game results in the formation of a structured set of expectations, a theoretical framework, which tells us which facts may be selected from experience and how these facts are to be shaped.[42]

The teacher's knowledge is a system of activity from which he derives certain propositions regarding the world—a system of activity from which the student will eventually be able to create information himself, thereby enabling him to dispense with the teacher. The teacher does not simply transfer X from himself to his students, he draws his students into a web of belief out of which knowledge is constructed. There are two language games into which the student is initiated: the discipline and its texts and classroom life. For the student to become a participant in these language games he must acquire certain facts regarding the nature of the discipline and the nature of classroom life that will enable him to make the appropriate moves in those language games. I shall refer to those language games as discursive universes. The moves in the game are interpretive strategies, and teaching is a system of activity involving the construction of meaning within particular interpretive frameworks. The frameworks are not directly transmitted. A does not teach a framework X to B. Nor is the discursive universe visible. But it is precisely in discourse that student and teacher meet, and in the narratives and stories enabled by the discourse that they find meaning.

Discussions of both the what and the how of teaching are incomplete. The matter of desire must not be neglected. The teacher teaches for some reason. Steven Unger examines the puzzle of desire by taking us to Roland Barthes' classroom. Here, Unger says, one sees clearly that teaching is an act of love, a sexual act in that its end is generative. Barthes, says Unger, is the professor of desire. And just what does he desire? The teacher seeks through his love to unite two loved objects—the student and the word. From this union comes the world. The teacher seeks nothing less than to create the world.[43] He does so by drawing his students into a system of interpretive activity that will enable them to speak together, to inhabit the same universe of discourse. This is an act of love employing the arts of persuasion. The practice of teaching is the practice of the art of rhetoric. The question for feminist pedagogy is, whom does the offspring, the world, resemble?

That pleasure and desire are the intimate companions of knowledge seems right. But again we are presented with a logocentric, a peculiarly masculine portrait, of desire. Desire is expressed in the discourse of philosophical idealism. All, in reminiscence of the primary narcissism during the period of pre-Oedipal attachment, is assimilated to the self. The world becomes expressible and encounterable only as an expression of subjectivity. Like the desire to call things by their proper names, to "say what we mean," the desire for world out of word is an attempt to dominate a maternal substitute. Just as the mother, during the moment of primary narcissism gives one to one's self in her gaze, the world, in mirroring subjectivity, is a speculum of the self and of the specular mother. The tension anchoring all the oppositions is the tension between desire to retreat to the maternal gaze and the need to look away. The world is a mirror of the self. The word is that which binds the self to the world. This is the son's desire and not the daughter's.

Plato understands desire very well. A master of logocentric rhetoric, he begins the *Phaedrus* by arguing that rhetoric reduced to disinterested application of technique, is rhetoric debased.[44] In the first section of the dialogue, Phaedrus tells Socrates of the substance of a speech he has just heard delivered by the sophist Lysias. Lysias claimed that one should surrender oneself only to those who are not in love and never to those who are. There are several reasons adduced in support of this recommendation. All of these relate to the central observation that the lover is ruled by passion to the extent that he himself often describes his condition as a sickness or a folly. He suffers from being out of control. The nonlover is always regulated by reason, in control of himself, and so will in all things work to increase the profit of those who act on his judgment and advice.

Socrates replies in, for him, typical fashion by defining love. Love is a kind of desire. He then explores all of the unhealthy, destructive desires—domination, contempt, condescension—to reach Lysias' conclusion that the nonlover, therefore, must possess all of the virtues opposite to those destructive desires. This is logocentric thinking in its crudest form. The absence of one thing implies the presence of its opposite.

We are not surprised, however, when Socrates immediately confesses a reservation. He is, after all, anything but crude. We know, as Phaedrus seems temporarily to have forgotten, that Socrates never settles so comfortably into any conclusion but that he is apt soon to discover himself mistaken. But, says Socrates, is love not a god, and how can that which is inspired by the divine be evil? Now Socrates suggests a distinction—that between the evil lover, a seducer merely, and the noble lover, the true lover. This is the best of seduction. I do not read Socrates' desire as Other to my own. He seems to express me, to mirror my own desire. My desire is then submerged in his. My relationship to Socrates, too, is a specular one. Socrates represents for me, my desire, by taking his own and presenting it as mine.

In Lysias' talk the lover had been represented as mad, as suffering a disturbance of the soul, and the nonlover as sane. Socrates invokes here the notion of a divine madness and proclaims "the superiority of heaven-sent madness over manmade sanity." There is a notable difference between madness arising from human ailments and "a divine disturbance of our conventions of conduct." While the two kinds of madness may often appear indistinguishable, the noble, or divinely-inspired lover joins passion for a loved one with seeking after wisdom. He is the professor of desire. Whether a lover is an evil seducer or noble depends on the nature of the god whose follower he is. The noble lover is a disciple of the god Truth. Socrates has discovered the transcendent One to which the Many must submit.

In the second part of the dialogue Socrates reveals that his discussion of the lovers is a metaphor for writing and speaking, for the practice of the art of persuasion. Phaedrus claims that the orator need not understand what is truly just; he need know only what is thought to be just by those in power for it is on this that persuasion depends. Socrates responds by saying that unless the orator understands what is truly just, he is in danger of becoming an evil speaker, one who tries to persuade his listeners that what is evil is good and what is good is evil.

The function of rhetoric, Socrates says, is to influence men's souls, and men can be influenced for good or for evil. The false dialectician, the speaker who influences for evil, mistakes certain skills for the art of rhetoric. He then compares the art of rhetoric with the art of medicine. Just as the doctor must understand the nature of the thing he treats, so must the speaker understand the nature of speaking. If the speaker does not have the same understanding of his art as the doctor has of his, the speaker can say, "I have the skill of speech, but one mustn't believe all that one is told."

Ignorance of the difference between understanding and skill leads men to elevate the merely plausible over the true. Socrates show the effect of this in pointing to the law courts. In the courts, he notes, even facts are thrown out when they do not comport with probability. This is the most grievous error into which the nonlover is likely to fall, confusing as he does his skill in using the techniques of persuasion with the goodness or truthfulness of that to which he is trying to persuade others.

When we set out to teach others we set out to change them, to persuade them to a point of view. Perhaps it is not overstating to say, uncomfortable as it may make us to say it, that the function of teaching is to change the souls of men (and women). That such is our aim must be admitted if we allow that our disciplines represent ways of seeing and recommend ways of being in the world, and that to initiate students into our disciplines is to bring them to different ways of seeing and being. We persuade them, when we are successful, to accept interpretations (ideally to construct interpretations of experience) which were not only previously unavailable to them but which may conflict with readings of experience previously settled on. Thus when we begin thinking of teaching as the practice of rhetoric we confront a moral problem.

It will no longer do simply to distinguish the skills and activities of teaching from those of other activities, useful though it may be to do so. We need still to distinguish good from bad teaching. Bad teaching can and often does mean something other than failure of student achievement or misapplication of skill. Another way in which we can be bad teachers is by teaching our students bad things. Humans learn, and by implication are taught, to be racists, fascists, and misogynists. The judgment that some teaching is good teaching amounts to more than an observation that certain skills were employed toward some end or that some end was achieved. When we consider the moral dimension of teaching, "knowing what to do" is phenomenologically indistinguishable from "knowing why." It becomes a matter of moral justification.

The disposition to teach springs from a commitment to initiating others into interpretive frameworks believed to be worthwhile, good, even sometimes true. Scheffler and Peters have criticized the Rylean perspective precisely because it cannot be made to accommodate the ethical dimensions of teaching.[45] And yet if the teacher is to be a noble lover, to paraphrase Socrates, a "true teacher," one worthy of being heeded, his passions must be joined to the pursuit of wisdom. If passion is not joined to the pursuit of wisdom, if the teacher looks only to his skill and to its results, he may say as does the false dialectician, "I know how to teach, but one must not believe everything one learns."

For us what does the pursuit of wisdom amount to? How do we ascertain the true nature of our texts? From where comes our authority to persuade, our warrant for believing that we are noble lovers and not evil seducers? We have not the authority of divine inspiration available to Socrates. Once we relinquish the objectivist metaphysics chased off by Ryle and others, the pursuit of Truth becomes an idle pasttime. Besides, we know now that there's more than one way to make love.

The moral nature of our enterprise against the background of a world view that no longer admits of appeal to divinity as a source of certainty in secular matters renders our authority as teachers problematic. That teachers do perceive their authority as problematic has become abundantly clear to me not only from my own thinking but from that of my student teachers as well. I am regularly appealed to to tell them what right they have.

> Making up a test—who am I to make up a test? Talking with John about it. About understanding yet not really fully understanding why a person gets a B, B+, or B−. Never understanding as a student why a B+ and not an A−, but an A− is so much better. A B+ is not a B− —it's better—it's nicer and a B− is not a C. How much of it depends on your mood? Am I as objective as I can be? Is it possible to be as objective as I want to be? (Student Journal)

The student teachers I work with are seniors and fifth-year MAT students at a small northeastern liberal arts college. These are among the few students at the university in any one year who choose teaching as a profession; most follow in their parents' footsteps and choose more lucrative and prestigious careers. It's a radical choice for my students. They make it for reasons which they confess, apologetically, to be "idealistic."

One of the first things I ask students to do in their teaching seminar is to imagine themselves teaching and to describe a particular situation. Their projections of these scenes disclose two things: a delight in and commitment to their subjects, and total ignorance of the fact that their high school experiences are not representative. Part of the anxiety of teaching begins when one acknowledges difference, when one recognizes one's own unrepresentativeness. The tension is the result of the persistent inclination to assimilate all experiences to one's own.

In their initial narratives, the student teachers imagine themselves as egalitarian and nonauthoritarian, friends to their students, understanding and supportive. They imagine their students choosing to read and construct a Renaissance masque rather than memorizing Shakespeare, enacting a revolution rather than taking notes from a book or a lecture, doing independent research on self-generated topics, translating literature into dance rather than writing about it. They imagine their students as themselves, already formed and with their tastes and dispositions.

The actual teaching experience is like the long-anticipated party which turns into a disaster. Many of the students at many of the schools in which my student teachers are placed are members of low-income farming families. Many of those above age 16 remain in school only so that their families can continue to receive Aid for Dependent Children. They begin a workday at 4 a.m. with farm chores and must return home immediately after school to work on the farm. Schooling is a priority neither for them nor their parents. They claim it is irrelevant to their present or future lives. They read poorly, sometimes not at all, are ignorant of most of the things a middle class student takes for granted, and are interested primarily in dating, hunting, and sports. Some of their teachers have long ago abandoned any ambition to teach them more than the "basics."

The student teacher who begins a lesson with, for example, the goal of helping students to develop a connoisseur's delight in Tolkein's use of language is first astonished by his students' ignorance and willed invulnerability to the charms of literature. His astonishment soon gives way to alternating moments of remorse and anger. At this moment he discovers that his lessons were projections of his own desire. He is hurt by his students' failure to give himself back to himself in their responses. The mirror returns nothing; its surface is undisturbed. He is bewildered by his inclinations to insist in the face of his commitment to a view of teaching which seems to forbid both anger and insistence.

In his education courses the student teacher has dedicated himself to the conviction that education should be meaningful and useful to students, that course content should reflect the concerns of adolescent life, that education should be based on free choice, and that, therefore, student choice must be honored. But the literature teacher loves his literature; he finds himself in it. He will feel successful when he feels the self he finds in that literature affirmed by his students' similar responses. To let them be wholly Other is to threaten his integrity, to deny his subjectivity in their refusal to reflect it. He believes that his own relationship to literature bestows significance on his life, on a life. But he can *know* this only if it is given back to him in the students' gaze.

My social studies teacher has chosen his field, more likely than not, from the conviction that students must learn to confront and think critically about the dilemmas of modern life. Moreover, he is pretty sure that he knows the choices a critical thinker will make because he is certain that he knows what choices ought to be made. My social studies teacher quickly discovers his students to be highly critical: they are critical of ERA, gun legislation, nuclear freezes, the right to choose abortion, etc. The teacher finds he must orient himself to the coordinates of his own desire and his political commitments.

> What right do I have? Here I am sitting up here on the Hill just because my father has a lot of money. Sitting around talking about democracy and morality and art and stuff and then thinking I can go out and decide for other people and tell them what they should think. (Student Journal)
> What good is it? They're right. Why should they care about independent clauses or symbols of death in Poe? What kind of stupid question—what does death look like? Who cares? Why should they even be here?
> Who do I think I am? (Student Journal)
> I really believe (I think) that I want my students to write their own thoughts. But then how can I punish them with a low grade when

they do? How do I know that I'm not just disagreeing? If I believe
that everyone has something valuable to say and that there are no
right and wrong answers in literature, what makes my thoughts
and feelings more "right" than theirs? How can I criticize? I say I
want them to discover their own feelings, and then I find myself
not liking what they discover so I'm critical and I start suspecting
them of not being honest. It's what I've always hated in lit.
courses. How can everything be equally valid and some things be
wrong? (Student Journal)
This emphasis I want to place on individual interpretation—how
can this possibly be considered "education"? After all, most of my
educational life has been spent rephrasing someone else's ideas, so
where do I get off undoing all this. (Student Journal)

Authority hurts. But some of us suffer more than others.
These are my problems too. Perhaps they were my problems first.
In the grammar of human relationships, it is entirely possible that
these student teachers are responding to my expression of my
desire. Their response enables me to project my own desire and
my own anxiety beyond myself. In moving beyond myself, I move
into the world of public discourse and legitimate my desire. They
and I are now members of the same community. We speak
together. I hear my voice in their notebooks, just as I hear Ryle's
voice in my own writing.

In the world of teaching, we all believe that some things are
truer, better, more valuable than others. We choose to teach those
things. We make judgments. At the same time, all of our reading
and our study seems to lead us straight into relativism. My
students are at home, *intellectually*, with the notion that the
structure and content of knowledge, whether scientific, social, or
aesthetic, is socially and historically conditioned, rooted in an
interested and subjectively apprehended world view. I and others
have helped them furnish their intellects with such ideas.
Deprived of a world in which the "merely subjective" is clearly
demarcated from the "objective," the entire world collapses easily
onto the pole of subjectivity. Since we have grown up believing
authority to derive from "objectivity," the displacement of
objectivity leaves little warrant for authority. We hear our students
say so often, "Well, but it's all just what someone thinks." And
we have taught them that despite our own desires.

In a world of unstable meanings, justification fits awkwardly.
For justification implies a court of appeal, and it is difficult to

know what we should appeal to. Teachers are in something of the same situation as poststructural literary critics.

Teachers and critics both interpret texts and communicate their interpretations in narrative form. Both teachers and critics are engaged in producing communities of readers who share their interpretations, in trying to persuade others to accept their beliefs. But what makes one interpretation better than another? Why is my reading of a text to be taken more seriously than that of my student? For literary critics these questions are not so urgent, of course, as they are for teachers. For teachers interpret not only texts, but all of classroom life, the students themselves, and these interpretations become models of a life.

In *Is There A Text In This Class?*, Stanley Fish[46] ventures to answer just such questions. The book's title has the following history.

At the conclusion of the first class meeting of the semester, a female undergraduate approaches the professor (not Professor Fish) with the question: "Is there a text in this class?" The professor, assuming that she had come in late, informs her that it is the *Norton Anthology*. Her response cues him to the fact that her question was very different from the one he heard. She said, "No, no. I mean in this class do we believe in poems and things, or is it just us?" Now Fish's colleague gets the point and rises to do battle: "Oh, I see. You're one of Fish's victims. Yes, there are poems; they have meanings, and, furthermore, I'm going to tell you just what those meanings are."

This anecdote does more than point out the humorous consequences of a theoretical disagreement among the English department faculty at Johns Hopkins. It shows how much stage setting is required for even a seemingly obvious question to be understood correctly. Fish argues that that is because the student's question has no meaning in itself, just as a literary text has no meaning in itself. In tracing genetically the exchange between student and professor, Fish demonstrates that the professor's eventual understanding of the question occurred because he was able to replace one interpretive framework with a more adequate one. He had interpreted the question first within an institutional framework. His reply to the student's question occurs within the context of a setting, "first day of class, university business." His eventual response was situated within the context of literary theory and a history of disagreement between himself and a particular colleague regarding matters of interpretation. He was able also to resignify the student. Her identity in his eyes shifted from "student seeking information" to "one-of-Fish's-victims" as the interpretive framework of the entire exchange shifted. A good deal of history and expectation guaranteed this exchange.

Fish's general position regarding critical work is that a text must be understood as an experience producing particular conventional effects in the reader rather than as "a repository of extractable meanings." Since the reader is a member of an interpretive community in possession of shared interests and assumptions, it usually *appears* that unimpeachable evidence for interpretation is to be found in texts. Fish argues that when we agree in our interpretations of a text, we agree on strategies for producing that text. Common strategies produce similar readings. At issue in disagreement is how one *ought* to read a text. The proper focus of the critic, then, is the reader. The question is what does a text do to a reader and how does it produce its effects? Critics answers these questions by taking themselves as a representative readers, just as teachers take themselves as representatives of their cultures.

Fish refers to his model as a "persuasion model." Whether he turns out to be a seducer or a noble lover, a good or an evil speaker, remains to be seen. One can see in the contrast between persuasion and demonstration precisely how literary theory may be useful in thinking about teaching.

> . . . Critical activity [or teaching] is controlled by free-standing objects in relation to which its accounts are either adequate or inadequate [under the demonstration model]; in the other critical activity is constitutive of its object. In the one model the self must be purged of its prejudices and presuppositions so as to see clearly a text that is independent of them; in the other, prejudicial or perspectival perception is all there is, and the question is from which of a number of equally interested perspectives will the text be constituted.[47]

Critical paradigms, understood within a persuasion model, appear to be entities rather like Wittgenstein's language games. The paradigm makes it possible to pick out facts in support of interpretations, but only because an interpretive framework has already been assumed. We cannot raise the question whether critics will lead us to believe what is false true and what is true false. Nor can we raise the question of whether we can trust them.

The image of teachers and researchers as critics and connoisseurs has been much used and useful. Teaching models and paradigms are constitutive of classroom reality and of facts about students in that same way that critical paradigms or interpretive frameworks are constitutive of literary texts. The same relationship holds between the methodologies and the canons of the disciplines we teach and their content. If we adopt Fish's persuasion model or one like it, we aim to create communities of readers. We intend that our students take for their own our methods of producing texts in order that their readings should be similar to ours. A teacher is more interested in agreement in interpretation. Now, the business is revealed in all of its riskiness. Seduction and noble loving may turn out not to be so clearly distinct. "What right do I have?"

Of course, there is always the possibility of simply ignoring the question. Far too much of the talk about teaching does. Passion and engagement are simply denied. A singular achievement of certain social science discourses, in which texts about teaching have been dictated, has been the purging of passion and authority from our thinking about teaching. The language of the social scientist is the language of the nonlover. This language dominates; it seduces with its fantasy of a knowledge of control. The logic of domination in such discourses operates in precisely the same way as in the rhetoric of Lysias' nonlover.

To be sure, there is also a good deal of wise, generous, passionate, and persuasive writing about teaching. And it has made us uncomfortable. For to relinquish a demonstration model, as such writing invariably does, seems to put the world at risk and our authority in it. In denying objective privilege to any point of view it seems that we lose the right to a point of view. Fish is convinced that we lose nothing at all:

> We have everything that we always had—tests, standards, norms, criteria of judgment, critical histories and so on. We can convince others that they are wrong, argue that one interpretation is better than another, cite evidence in support of interpretations we prefer; it is just that we do all those things within a set of institutional assumptions that can themselves become objects of dispute. Rather than a loss, however, this is a gain, because it provides us with a

principled account of change and allows us to explain to ourselves
and to others why, if a Shakespeare sonnet is only 14 lines long,
we haven't been able to get it right after four hundred years.[48]

It may allow us to explain why, when we have demonstrated
so much to be true about teaching and learning, we have been
unable to get it right. Is it true that we are no worse off than we
were? Is it possible that we are better off? Does such a theory save
our appearances?

It is difficult for teachers to be as sanguine as Fish. Perhaps
critics' authority does derive from and is predicated on their being
"ideal readers," the image of what it is to read for less adept
members of the community. Their readings are legitimate because
they embody the institutional assumptions which permit the
enterprise to proceed. What happens if we think of teachers as
"ideal readers" as I suppose we must if we would extend the
analogy? Perhaps the rhetorical force of teaching is dynamically
similar to that of literary criticism. But the ethical complications are
more profound, I think. In the first place, less adept readers than
teachers do not have the same freedom to disagree as do readers
of literary criticism. Teachers must be critical of themselves and
their own practices in a way that critics need not be. Their
practices have political consequences whether they will them or
not. Critical practices may, but they need not.

Still, so compelling is the romance of reason, so vigorous its
claims, we cannot but believe we can get it right. It seemed simply
to be a matter of giving up a small thing—certainty. But all would
not be lost. For reason could provide a regulative rule. Plato's
hyperrationality and the political oppression it implies could be
replaced with something like Stephen Toulmin's "good reasons"
approach to ethical judgment. Rather than concentrating on
content we concentrate on the function of ethical decisions. The
function of ethical decisions is to bring us nearer to an ideal
society, one in which harmony among all interests is attained. We
can determine, says Toulmin, whether a practice is worthy of
adoption by asking whether it would "genuinely lead to deeper
and more consistent happiness" for everyone.[49] When good
reasons can be provided for an action, that action can be justified,
and good reasons are clearly discernible. Then, just as literary
critics do not lose a profession by denying free standing and
independent texts, so too moral philosophers have work to do

even without metaphysics. Strategies and methods are then the object of study.

When I began working on the problem as a new and inexperienced, and conventionally educated, university teacher, I proposed that we, as teachers, become critics of our own practice by thinking of our practices as textual and by imagining ourselves as student-readers of those texts. I offered two questions to start such a project: What does this work do to readers? And, should we want to affect readers in the ways that we do? Interpretation for teacher-critics-of-their-own-practice becomes ethical interpretation. We become interpreters of our own rhetoric.

I began then to work with my student teachers in developing classroom narratives, exegeses of those narratives, and finally criticisms. Each student began by providing the rest of us in the seminar with a written narrative description of a lesson, detailing intentions, methods, student responses, etc. As the rest of us read, we kept in mind several questions. We noted first our prereflective responses to the narrative. Then we asked ourselves how the narrative produced its effects. We tried to imagine ourselves as the students for whom these lessons were intended and to imagine then the effects on us. We proceeded by determining the author's possible latent expectations and institutional assumptions. We asked "Who is the ideal reader of this text?" We looked for narratives in which interests seem to be harmonized, in which all are helped and none are hurt.

I was not long satisfied with this approach. I understood even then that I was still in the grip of relativism despite my resolve not to be paralyzed by it. Fish assures us that everything is fine because although relativism may provide delightful intellectual entertainment, no one can *be* a relativist. An obvious difficulty is that a narrative is not the thing itself. Nor does refinement in interpretation or judgment entail anything in the way of action. Perhaps no one can *be* a relativist. That means that ideas have no cash value. It means that we may all be seducers.

For all of the time that I have been teaching a philosophy of education course, I have been frustrated by my students' failure to comprehend the fatal defect of relativism—that one cannot be a relativist. It was so clear when Stanley Fish pointed it out to me. My students are more savvy than I. They have always understood that intellectual discussion has precious little to do with being or acting. I learned this only recently and serendipitously. Something

I said in a class elicited the enlightening explanation. I and my students had been going around for some time on the question whether it's wrong for anyone to hold certain beliefs. The students insisted that it was not. I was certain that it is. All of us were exasperated. It was obvious to me that the students understood what they were committing themselves to logically. They even understood with a degree of sophistication that brought them to cultural relativism. "It would be wrong for one of us, but not for one of them to support [genocide] etc." Finally a student said, "Look, it's just opinions, thoughts, ideas. You can *think* anything you want to as long as you don't *do* it. Sure it's okay to *think* genocide is all right. You just shouldn't *commit* it." So much for the possibility of a moral education as long as our education is an education only in ideas and texts.

4

Teaching the Text

This book was begun longer ago than I knew when I first proposed to write it. I think I had not yet begun school since the event I am about to report occurred on a weekday. I believe that because my mother was ironing in the kitchen while my sister and I played. My father was nowhere in evidence—probably he was at the construction site where he was then employed or it might have been the Pepsi-Cola bottling plant he worked at then. It was an overcast and drizzly day, the sort of day when the unshaded bulb in the overhead fixture seems to emerge from a fog. The world seems condensed to the points occupied by bodies and objects. In memory I see my young mother, only half my present age, her auburn hair in a ponytail, dressed in a blue flannel shirt, long tails hanging out over her dungarees. We called blue jeans dungarees then. I hear the breath expelled from the iron as it slides along the sleeve of a dampened shirt. The kitchen is alive and warm with the smell of steam and soap, and the music from the radio infuses all of the other sounds and sights and smells. My mother loved country and pop music and sang along. My sister and I thought she had the most beautiful voice in the world. On this morning in my memory I'm listening to a song by the Ames Brothers—"You Can't Go Back to Constantinople"—as I tug and push my sister around the greenish gray linoleum. Teaching her to dance I called it. And then I listened to the lyrics: "You can't go back to Constantinople 'cause it's Istanbul."

I asked my mother what those words meant, and she told me

about Turkey. As she talked, I conceived a fear both deeper and more enduring than my fear that the Russians would someday murder all of the adults in the U.S. and send all of us children to orphanages in Russia. I immediately began to worry that it could happen, somehow, someday—that I would be away from home, at my grandmother's or somewhere—and someone would change the name of my street. And if that happened, I suddenly knew, I would never see my mother or my sister again. You can't go back to Constantinople.

I call that moment my introduction to philosophy. At that moment I was struck by the appearance of something which had been there all along but which now came forward, standing out—sharply, insistently—against its familiar background. Long aware, as only children, philosophers, and writers are, of the power of language to make things real, I suddenly apprehended the significance of that knowledge in everyday life. It is a moment which, however, must be submerged and repressed in the practice of philosophy, as we quickly learn in our introductory courses. What is repressed in our paradoxes and syllogisms and treatises and arguments is that the meaning of language and its relation to thought and reality is in fact an expression of our anxiety about the reliability of a world that may hurt us and an anxiety over the trustworthiness of language and its speakers. If language is so powerful and so capricious, I may find myself alone in a strange world. It is precisely that fear that haunts Western philosophy at least since Descartes and marks the literature of the modern age.

When I was eleven years old I became a religious philosopher, and I exercised questions of morality and eternity vigorously and enthusiastically. The high point of that career I achieved while sweeping the kitchen floor one Saturday morning. I was asking myself my usual questions, asking them really of the Bible stories and verses I was given to memorizing at the time. Doubt was asserting itself, whispering, as it does under the notes of certainty of all philosophies. All of a sudden I experienced a revelation—an experience that I would learn my sophomore year in college to call "ineffable" and "self-validating." All of a sudden I understood everything. My mother was still in bed reading as she usually was on Saturday mornings. I recall that I did not even pause to lean the broom in a corner but carried it with me as I ran up the stairs to tell my mother everything I knew and understood. I found that I could not; there were no words for that experience. While I no longer recall even the emotional tones of my epiphany, I do recall that it stifled the whispers of anxiety in much the way the Descartes' apprehension of God's existence enabled him to intuit his own and that of the material world.

By the time I was fifteen, I was an atheist, a moral relativist, and a nihilist, and I no longer spoke to my mother if I could help it. We no longer spoke the same language. I dressed in black, pierced my ears and read Kerouac and Ginsburg. I read Nietzsche and Camus and Sartre. I learned to smoke cigarettes, drink coffee and curse casually in the Howard Johnson's restaurant across from school. The books I read were full of girls like me, or such as I hoped to be, girls my mother did not approve of. For hours I languished and burned in a fever of talk with the irreverent and melancholy boys who had, I thought, the souls of artists. I wrote passionate poetry full of despairing love and rank with the failure of humans to comprehend each other. By that time, I had embraced, made a virtue, of the anxiety that had animated my first excursions in the realm of philosophical idealism—the anxiety attending separation from home and mother. But more important I had repudiated the literal and embodied center of that fear—my mother. I had become signatory to a symbolic contract in which one agrees to take language as all there is or is to be known of the world and of one's self even as one fears that one's inscription of one's self in language is an inscription on a magic writing slate. Peel back the page and all of self and the world vanish.

These stories adumbrate the theoretical and practical concerns which have sometimes animated and sometimes afflicted my intellectual and pedagogical practice. They raise for me questions of authority, in truth and in relationships. Trust and doubt and the need for both are elements of my education. The need for talk, the reality of an Other whose attention confirms my experience and the fear of being unable to speak truly or of being misunderstood appears as a critical theme in my stories. All are concerned with the power of language and its vicissitudes and with the uses to which language may be put. Taken together all three of these stories develop a picture of the daughter's estrangement from her mother through language. They develop a picture of repudiation of the mother. They are also a beginning from which to trace a daughter's journey among institutional discourses and the double consciousness required of her as she frames the world within them.

In the first story, the child discovers that the word has power, that the word can divide her from her mother and sister forever. (The child was nearly middle-aged before she understood the significance of that discovery.) The crucial phrase is, "that I would be away from home . . ." Of course, the child could have relieved that anxiety by staying at home always. This child settled on a more typical solution and became a philosopher instead. The second story is an ironic one. While its overt content is belief, it actually retails the dawning of the perception of the limits of language. This one is truly a cultural learning since it prepares the child to enter a world of shifting meanings and texts, a world in which the dominant theoretical posture is that of the skeptic. I had no language to tell my mother, she whose agreement would confirm my experience, what that experience was. My mother, though, was reading. The third story finds the mother and the mother's language completely rejected. A young girl creates herself from the images and representations provided by her fathers and brothers. She renounces communication with her mother transferring her longing for communion to a romantic sexual Other. But that Other, the romantic hero of her books and poems and philosophies, the offspring of the patriarchal imagination, has taught her that impossibility, has taught her what Stanley Cavell calls "the wisdom of skepticism."[50]

These stories give us a fairly standard account of female psychological development and illustrate nicely the fluctuations between issues of separation and attachment. They also furnish an account of education in general and of female education specifically.

When we teach we talk. We communicate. Students may be thought of as communicants. In philosophers' terms they become initiates into certain language games. They become masters of discourse. According to the OED to communicate is to "make common" or to "give a share of." Those who communicate impart information or knowledge. They tell. These usages of the word all have a generally mental reference. "Communion," says the OED, has principally a spiritual reference having also to do with sharing or holding in common, with mutual participation. But "communion" has to do also with an organic union of persons. My language is a metonymical expression of my life as I find myself, through language, through knowledge sharing a world in common with others.

In Chapter 1, I said that language is always compensatory. Speech redeems the loss of the maternal body; through speech we generate a series of substitutes for her body. But I also said that the order of magnitude, even that the sort of compensatory effect required, is different for males and females, that men and women, because their relationship to the maternal body is different, also bear different relationships to language. For women that body is not entirely lost. Women carry the mother in the form of their own bodies for all of their lives.

The radical difference which defines the relationship between men and the mother is expressed in a language based on bipolarity, on bipolar sexual difference, and on presence and absence. The problem of language is the problem of Otherness. The problem of the Other is different for women, since the original Other has a body like her own. If discourse is grounded only in the male experience of Otherness, then a woman can only speak as Other to herself. She is beside herself. Lacan said that any theory of the subject is masculine. The speaking subject is necessarily male.[51] The unitary subject which takes up its position in language, then, always takes up a male position. The unitary "I" is the first in a chain of substitutes for the self first known in the mother's gaze. That first self is a body subject, continuous with the maternal body and so unknowable because of the taboo on the maternal body, on *knowing* the maternal body. The speaking subject has a unity denied the body; it is continuous with and wholly available only to itself. It depends on the absence of the maternal body; it demands the subjugation of all bodies. Hence, for Lacan, the impossibility of female knowledge or of a female speaking subject. The stories I told at the start of this chapter touch on just that impossibility, I think. For central to all three of them is silence between mother and daughter as daughter moves into the institutionalized discourses of the public world. The connection which I was terrified of losing could not be meant in the face of the power of the word.

"If he can speak he has got something to say," says Wittgenstein.[52] With this premise, Wittgenstein begins what he calls his grammatical investigations, investigations into the relationship between expressing and responding, between speaking and being. His search, as Cavell demonstrates, is a search for community, a search to discover who is implicated by him in his expressions.[53] He proceeds by adducing criteria of meaning.

When he asks what we say, or what we should say, he is making neither empirical generalization nor predication; nor is he making a normative claim. He extends an invitation. We may find that we do not say what he says; we decline the invitation. We are not members of the same community. "If a lion could speak he would be one of us," said Wittgenstein. That is, if he could speak to us. Lacan might say, "When a woman can speak, she is one of us." She has accepted the invitation. But at what cost? Language, in Wittgenstein's reading, is what draws us into the body politic. In Lacan's reading, it draws us away from the maternal body. More powerfully, it exiles the maternal body. And yet, as the elusive and obscure object of desire, the maternal body is a spectre haunting language. The maternal body is the literal object of desire, and all the world as we know it, a figurative substitute. Still, as women we know it differently. We know the world in some sense as exiles from our own bodies.

Some are fond of saying, "I don't teach English, etc., I teach children." The equivocation is amusing, but it is nonetheless an equivocation. Certainly one teaches children. One also teaches subjects. When we teach we talk. We talk about something. Let us suppose that when I teach I act as a grammarian of the text. I investigate the relationship between its expressions and my own. Cavell says that as a grammarian of the text, I claim to speak representatively as a reader. I communicate, make common, give a share of my discoveries. I tell you what *we* do, what *one* does, how *one* reads by demonstrating what I do. In order for you to understand me, though, we must already hold a great deal in common. If you are to understand me, you must already be in a position to know what is written in the text before I read it. What we learn is always obvious. You can't go back to Constantinople. To teach is to express the subtleties and profundities of the obvious.

Obviousness is a matter of position. The conception of "position" I have in mind has both mental and physical coordinates. We cannot assume that men and women are in a position to know the same things since their relationship to language, to the spectral body and to the body politic is different. Since education has everything to do with our finding our positions in language, education must treat men and women differently within the range of the common interest which defines the educational project.

Just as we learn from our relative positions, so do we teach
from our relative positions. If position makes a difference both
politically and epistemologically, as I maintain it does, then
serious questions respecting the authority of teachers and texts are
raised. I turn now to a particular text directed toward teaching the
text and interrogate textual interpretations. I first read the text and
wrote an essay that became this chapter for a symposium on
Teaching the Text that I participated in with Madeleine Grumet,
Max van Manen, and William Pinar. For my purposes it is
important to note that I first read it with others, to do some work
with others. When I think about it now, I think of one/those
Russian nesting eggs with smaller and smaller dolls inside each
until you get to one that's almost invisible. The book itself is a
collection of lectures given in a university literature department.
But it is not just a collection of lectures. The authors of the text
were, in a sense, teaching about teaching to, presumably,
colleagues interested in reading about teaching about teaching,
while we were reading the text and writing about it to speak to an
audience interested, presumably, in hearing about reading a text
about teaching about teaching, a text that was to model what it
was about. I brought to the text the history embedded in the
stories with which I began this chapter. I also brought to it certain
questions regarding theory and relativism, language and authority, and readers and communities.

One of the purposes of Teaching the Text,[54] its editors tell us, is
"to make visible the criteria of teaching." They are not, it seems,
interested in standards or judgments, in good or bad teaching, but
in teaching as such. In this connection the question they pose is
what makes teaching different from other things the university
pays us for, specifically, what makes teaching different from
research? The reader is given to understand that the twelve
contributions to this volume will display the distinguishing
features of teaching—its criteria. Of course, we can speculate
about the reasons one may be interested in distinguishing
teaching from research, some honorable and others less so. If we
were not to distinguish the two activities in important ways, we
should be hard pressed to maintain our present university reward
system. The book actually achieves something quite different.

The pieces, taken singly and together, compel the overwhelm-
ing conclusion that the only differences between teaching and
research are matters of style and convention, and these differences

are dictated by consideration of to whom what is said is said. *The presence of different audiences changes the text.* This is a difference far more important than whatever differences may obtain between teaching and research. Position, inflection, orientation count for everything. That the editors do not make this perception part of their account is owing to the fact of mutual participation in certain presumptions which enable a common cultural conversation, those presumptions without which the cultural conversation could not be held, presumptions which will prevent my ever returning to Constantinople. The expression of those presumptions is the core of both teaching and research. We shall examine them.

In the lecture entitled "Hawthorne's Illegible Letter," Norman Bryson argues that Hawthorne was neither asserting the moral force of the community nor celebrating the rebellion of individual conscience, although such readings dominate the interpretations of previous generations of readers. He argues that *The Scarlet Letter* is important as a discontinuous text, one destructive of meaning, one which makes vivid to the reader the experience of "having meanings torn, slashed, and destroyed." As evidence he offers the inconsistency of characterization, the withholding of information from the reader. (Is the "A" on Dimmesdale's breast a delusion, a real self-inflicted wound, or a sign of the intrusion of supernatural forces? Hawthorne never tells us.) Hawthorne's intention, Bryson speculates, is to foil the reader's inclination to make the sort of Manichean ethical judgments that were the hallmark of Puritan culture. Such judgments are to be avoided because they proceed from an illusionary decoding of an intractable and illegible world text. A moral fiction in Bryson's universe is one which duplicates the illegibility of the world-text and manages to do so because the author maintains a position of ethical neutrality.

Tony Tanner, in his discussion of *Wuthering Heights*, locates the tragedy of Catherine Earnshaw and Heathcliff in their passion to "escape from grammar." They long to avoid "the essence of growing up." To grow up is to acquiesce in human separation, to recognize that we can know one another only indirectly, through symbol systems. Tanner directs our attention to what he reads as the significance of the incident in which the two throw one of old Joseph's pamphlets into the dog kennel. The dogs stand for raw existence, the pamphlets for civilization. Where, Tanner asks, would they put the dogs? They must come to a sad end because their desire for total communion imperils civilization itself. They would relate in some medium of raw existence, but raw existence must be locked up, enkenneled, and domesticated by the sociable forms of language. Tanner supports his reading by contrasting the narrative strategy of *Wuthering Heights* with that of *Jane Eyre*. I talked about his reading of *Jane Eyre* in different context in chapter 2. Jane, we recall, tells her own story. Hers is an autobiography through which, with each stroke of her pen, Jane insists on the integrity of her own unique identity and thereby asserts her claim on the sociable world. Catherine and Heathcliff are silent. Their story is a double translation, first through the voice of Nelly Dean, then through the pen of Mr. Lockwood. Tanner sees the storytellers as redeemers, the telling of the story as a redemptive act freeing future generations from the ghost of the original tragedy. At the conclusion of the novel, sitting in the sunshine, heads bent close together over a *book*, are Catherine Linton and Hareton Earnshaw.

If we read through the other pieces in the volume we detect striking similarities in position to the Bryson and Tanner teachings. Colin McCabe argues that typical "misreadings" of Milton have been propagated by critics who either mistook the relationship between language and subjectivity, or who, like T. S. Eliot, were so naive as to have conflated language with speech and sight. Milton's language, McCabe says, is to be heard as an activity which produces its own truth, thereby putting poetry on the same epistemological footing as science. Science becomes simply another activity productive of its own truth. Stern's reading of Musil's *Young Torless* interprets the young hero's complicity in acts of sadistic brutality, even in the face of the afflictions of his conscience, as provoked by the young man's awareness of the tenuous link between language and reality. Stern argues that Musil asserts finally the power of some inward and wholly aesthetic truth over the illegibility of reality. Sartre's *Nausea* is read as yet another excursus into the poverty- and disease-ridden slums of language and knowledge. Yet again salvation comes to us in an aestheticized experience. With Anita Kermode as guide, we follow Emerson on his quest for a pure interiorized landscape, one uncluttered by the excrescence of the human body with its false intimations of temporality. We are invited to witness Dorothy Richardson's attempts to write herself a life, attempts thwarted again and again by her failure to find a female sentence, the rhythms of which would express a female consciousness.

These readings are intelligent and intelligible. Their intelligibility tells us a great deal about the social world we inhabit, a great deal about our assumptions regarding language and knowledge, self and community, and particularly about our knowledge of other selves. Among all of the contributors, only Anita Kermode acknowledges that what we assume is pretty fearsome stuff. These readings, these teachings, position us in an unknowable, illegible universe, alone with our awesome power to read or to write it as we will. We, as readers or writers are omnipotent in a logocentric universe that exists nowhere but in our expressions of it. There seems no alternative to relativism. We may write, but we have no certain knowledge that what we write is true, no certain knowledge that the world we read is as we read it, and no certain connection to each other. We have no reason to *trust* each other. Perhaps we only seem to talk to each other. Each of us is adrift in seismic universe. At once powerful and helpless, we search for a writing to graft on to the narcissistic wound. Each of us, for all that we *really* know, really *know* is right at this moment seated before a fire, in his or her dressing gown, and dreaming. Or perhaps more horrifying: Each one of you is a cleverly constructed automaton created to deceive me into thinking that other beings like me inhabit the world. Or more horrifying still, I do not exist.

Who can mean such things, and to whom can they be meaningful? What are the relative positions of writer and reader, of teacher and student? Language, we have said, is compensatory. To speak is to generate a series of symbolic substitutes for an obscure, indeed an unnameable, object of desire. In listening and speaking we search for and locate the world and find our positions in that world, positions determined by our orientation to the original object for which the world we find in our language substitutes. That world is all that we have of each other, hence all that we have of ourselves.

Here knowledge and the body intersect even as the body is denied. The word transcends the world, becomes the world as substitute for the maternal body which first represents all that we know of the world. The first thing we know is that we are connected. The next thing we know is that we are separate, exiled from the maternal body into the insubstantial word. Cavell argues[55] that the tradition of skepticism which informs our culture

is attuned to this second knowledge. This is the wisdom of
skepticism. Coeval with this second knowledge is a primal desire
for connection, an unslakeable desire to be known by others, by
an Other. Our readings and speakings are expressions of this
knowledge and this desire. Says Cavell, other-minds skepticism
teaches us that there is no alternative to trust.[56]

Even at the moment of skeptical recognition, though, the
myth of skepticism denies our primal knowledge and excludes the
possibility of the trust it demands. The myth is a symbolic
substitution for the lost object and the lost connection. It promises
redemption through knowledge. Connection is transformed into
an epistemological problem, and is then denied epistemological
status. The primal knowledge of connection is banished from the
realm of knowledge because such knowledge cannot be encom-
passed within a logocentric universe. Literal knowledge must be
controlled by the figure; the literal maternal body disappears, is no
longer present to be desired. Desire alone persists. This is the
tragedy of patriarchy and logocentric thinking.

We insist that the limits of human knowledge can somehow
be surpassed or that we can know enough to accommodate
ourselves comfortably within those limits. Born of a tragic insight,
knowledge is ironically transformed into what Nietzsche some-
place referred to as "scientific optimism." This transformation
yields an illusion of power. And yet the dominant interpretations
of reality through which we all live in common are permeated by
the initial tragic knowledge. From the institutionalized discourses
of patriarchy, the first knowledge is banished. The price of exile
from the maternal body is exile of connection from the realm of
knowledge. We lose the literal world which might be a source of
comfort.

Women have always known this, of course. In *To the
Lighthouse*, Virginia Woolf makes Mr. Ramsey's idealism look
perfectly foolish as Lily Briscoe translates his Table into a
particular deal table, scraped and scrubbed and used in someone's
kitchen. (Of course, Mr. Ramsey would feel nothing so much as
confirmed in the knowledge that women have no capacity for
Ideas.)

Cavell argues that the material world skepticism so adequately
dispatched by ordinary language philosophy is an artifact of
skepticism, its tragic knowledge. He argues that the material
world is beyond doubt, although particular perceptions may be in

error, and that the scientific optimist has quite correctly demonstrated that questions regarding the existence of that world are pseudoquestions. But, says Cavell, the same is not true of other minds. The strategies and arguments which will do for demonstrating the necessity of the material world will not give us the existence of an Other, *like us.*[57] My husband may be a teenage werewolf, my friend and neighbor an alien invader. Here we say something exists, but we don't know what it is. The whole business comes down to a distrust of the literal body and a suspicion of its representations. The whole enterprise of philosophy comes down to finding a basis in certifiable, demonstrable knowledge for trust. What others *appear* to be can mislead. Moreover, what someone *says* may be an outright lie. The Other, this Other who gives me back to myself, may intend to deceive me for his own purposes. Just as the mother betrayed me by her absence, so is the possibility of betrayal always with me. And this may always be true. We come smack up against the limits of knowledge when the primal knowledge of connection is excluded from the realm of knowledge, and certainty becomes a matter of faith—hence a matter of anxiety.

Reading Tanner's reading of *Wuthering Heights* against this background, one must be touched by his insistence on the equation between adulthood and language. Against this background his neglect of the source of the storytellers' knowledge is not so curious as it might at first seem. Tanner, the optimist, looks for redemption in language. But in this story, redemption embodies its inverse. Not only does Nelly tell the tale to Lockwood, but one of Nelly's main functions in the story she retails is that of storyteller. And the stories she tells often have catastrophic consequences for the other characters. Furthermore, Nelly is in a position to know what other characters do not (sometimes by listening behind doors), and she gives and withholds information at her will. Her withholding from Catherine the fact that Heathcliff is in the room while Catherine is announcing her engagement to Edgar is only one such instance. Her interpretation of Catherine's fit following the fight between Edgar and Heathcliff as theatrical self-indulgence, and her consequent decision to leave Edgar in ignorance of his wife's state, are the immediate causes of Catherine's death. This servant, in the act of telling stories, exercises the greatest power. In the economy of storytelling, power is the prize. Lockwood, through whom

Nelly's story is refracted, is among the stupidest and vainest of men. He is a poseur of a romantic, self-aggrandizing to the last page. But there at the end of the novel, sitting in the sunlight with the young lovers, who are *reading*, is Nelly Dean—like Madame DeFarge, knitting—Lockwood beside her. I cannot imagine that scene without seeing a shadow move across the sun. Nor I suspect could Emily Brontë. The act of storytelling presumes the rightness of a particular choice, the choice to enter into the symbolic contract, a contract in which the price of social power is the immediate connection to the maternal body. The storyteller relinquishes maternal language and submits to paternal law. The power is expressed through symbolic language.

In support of her claim that men and women stand in different positions with respect to language, Homans gives a reading of *Wuthering Heights* similar to mine.[58] She finds in the figure of Lockwood, the representative male storyteller, one who writes out of a peculiarly male desire. His writing is a process of generating symbolic substitutes for the embodied and literal mother. She reminds us that Lockwood has fled to Yorkshire from the threat of the satisfaction of his romantic interest. He tells the reader that he had loved this lady until he seemed about to achieve his heart's desire. Then his ardor cooled. It is a common story. What Lockwood had loved was not the lady herself, but his representation of his relationship to her. Homans notes that all of Lockwood's writing about nature renders nature symbolically. Not coincidentally, nature *literally* menaces Lockwood's life. He loses his way in the storm and falls ill because the markers—the writing—on the road have vanished in the snow. The other storyteller, Nelly Dean, is *literally* a servant in the paternal order, and as such she is pledged to uphold that order. Only such a voice, Homans argues, permits Brontë to write. But Catherine herself embodies the female tragedy in all of its difference from that of the male. In choosing for the mother, Catherine herself dies immediately after giving birth. Catherine is eternally silent in the silent landscape of her childhood.

As Tanner claims, adulthood or maturity depends on entry into the symbolic order. Attending to Brontë's narrative strategies, Homans demonstrates that *Wuthering Heights* depicts this develop-mental fact and expresses the tragic nature of that requirement for the female. She notes that the text shifts back and forth between literal and figurative representation. She notes that Catherine is silent about her own story. About those times when Catherine is happiest, roaming the moors either alone or with Heathcliff, the text is silent. Catherine is *literally* in nature and, by association, with the mother. To speak of those times is to be out of them, to have lost them. To speak of them is to symbolize them. Nature is symbolized by Lockwood; Nelly would prefer to stay indoors. But Catherine, says Homans, would rather be in nature than write about it. In choosing nature over symbolization, she has chosen the mother. For, Homans argues, in the life of the text, the literal is structurally similar to nature in the life of the human.

The second Catherine, she who was born, significantly, in her mother's deathbed, represents the alternative female choice. We hear her enter adulthood. At a moment of loss she speaks nature symbolically. She reads nature, gives it meaning, and thereby banishes the mother. Many readers of *Wuthering Heights* have observed that nature appears almost as a character. Nature, like the mother, is silent; in culture she is written. When she is written she is controlled; her loss is compensated for. She is comprehended. Still, there is an excess over meaning, and it is there that we may speak the claims of female experience. At the end of *Wuthering Heights,* the paternal house—the Heights—stands empty except for the brooding Joseph. At Thrushcross Grange, the house associated with feminine culture,[59] the young Cathy, she who speaks her sadness, is about to become Earnshaw. In marrying Hareton she will redeem the maternal name.

Nature and the literal maternal are comprehended and yet continue to contest the claims of culture and sociability, the claims of reason and of the text. Over and over again they must be exiled to the territory of symbolization and condemned to a ghostly eternity of haunting. She, who in her muteness menaces the objects of speech, reveals only this: there is no alternative in human life to incompleteness, separation, and to the possibility of betrayal and misunderstanding. I think of Hamlet's awful discovery that the play, that language, reveals nothing. Reality is silent. The Other is opaque. We are thrown back on representation. This is the wisdom of skepticism. This is what literature teaches us. At the same time, literature teaches us, recalls us to that first knowledge of connection and thereby contests the futility and domination inherent in logocentrism. In doing so, literature helps to redraw the boundaries of the realm of knowledge and to contest the limits which deprive that first knowledge of authority.

In writing and in teaching we construct and maintain our identities. We also construct the reader and the student, the Other whose understanding will confirm us. Similarly, when we read, perhaps particularly when we read fiction (although I do not exclude the best of philosophy, history, and social science) we listen for the voice which seems to reach all the way to our experience, thereby confirming it. As Cavell says, in writing we seek those who speak representatively for us, and those for whom we speak representatively. Because of this, he says that all writing is the imparting of a political education. In our writing, our reading, and our teaching, we represent ourselves as members of a polis. He says that we do not represent new facts or certainties in our writing. We do represent our own positions.[60] The question of position leads us to the question of *who* is there to hear us. For only if we believe that our words reach directly to the experiences of others, can we know that we exist for others. All of our writing is a variation on that first cry in that first position of separation from the maternal body.

Well, who *is* there to hear it? How many times have we heard our teachers say, "Your bodies are here, but your minds are not?" In the optimist's compact with the symbolic order, the fate of the body is interesting. It disappears. (Think of the pale and scrawny scholar, poet, preacher who forgets to feed himself.) Let us entertain the converse assertion: our minds are there, but our bodies are not. I find that I cannot locate myself in the positions taken by the contributors to *Teaching the Text*. There are no bodies there toward which I might orient myself. There are I's but no You's. There are Ones and Readers, but no Me's. Still, mind consciousness, however much we protest, is known by its corporeal expressions—through voice, through gesture—as well as through ideas. To deny corporealness is to deny that which makes knowledge possible.

On one occasion I observed a student teacher on the day that he announced to his college-bound twelfth-grade class (the honors class) that for their next assignment they should choose a favorite poem, story, or essay to read aloud to the rest of the class. It was not to be an original composition or a recitation from memory. They were simply asked to read aloud. There was a general and very loud outcry. The panic nearly resulted in mutiny. The following day we asked these students to write paragraphs explaining their resistance. Without exception they mentioned fear of their classmates' ridicule. They were not worried about their classmates' possible scorn for the selections they might make. They were afraid of mispronouncing a word, of having a funny-sounding voice, of being dressed stupidly. They do not trust their bodies, alien things which might betray them. They do not trust each other, alien beings who might betray them. When we asked them during discussion why it seemed that they did not mind speaking from their seats, objected only to standing in the front of the room, it was clear from their responses that they did not feel *seen* when they were in their seats. They said that.

At the end of the discussion, we asked everyone to stand up. We then asked each person to make a circuit of the room, shake hands, and say, "How do you do," to every other person. The giggling awkwardness, hunched shoulders, pink cheeks, and averted eyes were predictable. That exercise became the basis of a discussion of trust and the relationship between trust and learning. We modified the speaking assignment. The students were directed to select pieces for reading that touched the problem of trust.

The point is that to minimize or deny the corporeality of knowing is to minimize or deny the possibility of knowing. I find it suggestive that we say we *feel* stupid or we *feel* that we understand. (I no longer require my students to substitute "think" or "believe" for "feel" in every case.) These expressions have bodily referents. I feel stupid. My skin reddens and prickles. My insides shrivel, and my eyes sting. I wish I were invisible. Or suddenly I know something. Now my skin tingles in expectation, feels live. The hairs on my arms and the back of my neck stand up. My heart seems to expand and fill my whole body. I may even smile. I feel powerful.

Clearly I overstated when I said that the bodies are not there. The body intrudes. It insists. I stammer; I blush; I sweat. I am fat or thin. The room is cold or too hot. I am thirsty. I need to go to the bathroom. I have a pimple on my chin. My stomach turns somersaults in apprehension that I might be called on. My stomach knows as well as I the humiliation of being wrong. My body's embarrassing presence renders me mute and expressionless. I am connected to my body.

Anyone who has thought seriously about our classrooms and curricula understands their an-aesthetics. The inhospitality of the physical, psychological, and intellectual spaces is intended to domesticate the body and to curb desire. In these spaces a transfer occurs. Madeleine Grumet has described the curriculum as a mechanism for delivering the child to father's world. She describes its function in contradicting the maternal claim and in contradicting the child's desire for the mother.[61] During the course of the delivery, which is of course a metaphor for the initial "delivery" from the mother's body, the body's position becomes metaphorized. We take positions figuratively from now on. But the body persists. It seems in the way. It seems in the way of communion. The body stands as a barrier to the meeting of the minds. The body imperfectly reflects our beautiful thoughts. The body betrays. The body is in the way of knowledge. Because of the body's indurateness we can speak only metaphorically and know only inferentially. Knowledge is a substitute for its own incompleteness. It is a substitute for its own original loss and its own unnameable desire. The figurative position, though, is an impossible one for the reader, the teacher, the writer, the student who would take up her position as female also. To stand just there, she must exclude herself, for her body will insist on resembling that of the first disappeared object—the maternal body. To know is to know the mother's absence.

Denial of the body is the paradoxical effect of an epistemology engendered of the body. The fate of the body inheres in a compensatory epistemology born not just of loss—*but of loss of the original experience of connection.* The prototype of body knowledge is childbirth. A mother, under ordinary circumstances, does not doubt that her child is hers. Had Descartes borne children Western philosophy might have followed a very different course. The father labors under no such conditions of certainty. Just as he might mistake the finch in his garden for some other bird, he might mistake his wife's offspring of another union as his own. A major system of custom and law permits the father to know (and to claim), more or less, his own children. Still, he can never be certain—not absolutely certain. Nor can he ever be absolutely certain that his wife has not betrayed him. He may list all that he knows about her, her dispositions and actions in the past. He may assure himself of her commitment, moral and otherwise, to monogamy. He may assure himself of her religious beliefs. He may mark down the dates of sexual intercourse and calculate the time of probable conception to the date of delivery. For all his labor, he will never achieve certainty. Paternity is textual.

Maternal knowledge menaces the authority of the paternal text. A feminine position potentially subverts the text. A system of philosophy has been erected on this primal uncertainty. Descartes' story is the father's. The skeptic's position is that of the father. Just as we cannot know that event A causes event B, constant temporal conjunction permits the inference. Just as a father cannot know his own child, certain conjunctions give him good enough reason to believe.

The problems we raise are not strictly or merely epistemological. They are political as well. The inference of paternity grants to the father certain property rights in his mate's children and certain property rights in his wife's body. His power over them is legitimate.

In our schools, in our disciplines, our arts and our corporations, the father's position, that of the skeptic, defines reality. That knowledge which is least dependent on the body, figurative and inferential knowledge, is the most esteemed. School knowledge is textual and authoritative. He who is its author exercises a legitimate power to construct, define, and circumscribe the world in his own figures. He who interprets—the teacher—inscribes his desire on the world. He is the priest, the scientist, the author, the teacher. He is the grammarian of the text and his relationship to it is one of privilege. He represents the limits and the terms of the cultural conversation.

Our cultural conversation unfolds in the register of desire. Knowledge is engendered of a double desire: the desire to know the mother, she-who-is-forbidden, and the father's to desire to know. She has the power, in her gaze, to give one back to oneself; she has the power to subvert the father's text. Since one can never really know what the mother knows, her power is alarming. It must be taken from her. She must become the blank page on which the cultural conversation is recorded.

That relationship to the mother and to knowledge is the male's. The desire which informs it is male desire. It is also the skeptic's. Translated into curriculum and pedagogical practice it becomes the paradigm for all that we do. It may seem odd to ground education in the skeptic's position, since that would appear to make teaching radically impossible. Just as the counting of days and the listing of attributes, the control of movement affords the father relative certainty, good enough knowledge, of his wife's children's legitimacy, so too our strategies of inference and figuration afford us a relative certainty. Our classrooms, too, are textual. Our testing and grading practices permit us to make inferences about things we can't really know. What we know and say about the bodies is more important than the bodies themselves. The teacher who acknowledges the inferential basis of her knowledge and her knowledge of her students inevitably confronts the ethical problems described in the preceding chapters.

The teacher-student relationship is not uncommonly represented as a conversation. Through this relationship students become participants in a cultural conversation. The teacher helps to initiate the student into that conversation. Teaching and learning unfold in the register of desire. Knowledge in the register of desire becomes a search for acknowledgment, for finding and forming oneself in the representations with which our world is written. But desire, assimilated as it has been to the phallus, is distinctly male.

A female teacher now has to investigate her own position with respect to that desire in order to find one that is distinctly her own. This is a difficult project. For the language we have is the language we have, and what we know is what we know. I do not believe that this language is totally inhospitable to female experience. If I believed that I could neither teach nor write this book. I do believe that the institutional workings of language and knowledge as they are described by such theorists as Lacan, do exclude that experience. What such writers leave out of account is that first knowledge of presence—the presence of an Other—and connection. A feminist pedagogy, or a feminist writing, asserts that presence and contests the privilege of the unseen, of the figure that replaces literal presence. The question of how to do that is the question of this book. This book is a strategy for answering that question. In telling stories we enact connection. Feminist pedagogy displays confidence in connection.

5

Practical Fictions

I understand that the dilemmas posed by the incompleteness of language are the dilemmas posed by human relationships. In other words I have come to read the apparent incompleteness in language as a tale of connection denied or subordinated. I have come to understand that by reading certain questions as personal statements. I rewrote this chapter about a year and a half ago. It was a revision of an essay that I wrote in 1985. During the period between 1985 and early 1987, I had exposed, or more properly had had exposed to me, through my responses to the work of my student teachers, my own anger and my ambivalence about my teaching and my writing both. I had come to understand that the crisis of authority I related in Chapter 3 was a self-description. I had apprehended my own desire to have my students believe me, share my vision of the world. This is no longer a matter of language, truth, and authority merely. It is a matter of who I am to others. It is a matter of my identity as well as theirs.

I teach because I want to change the world. And like Socrates, I believe that we teachers have it in our power to act on the world for evil or for good. That was why I fell so thoroughly for Socrates once. Because I believe the student who told me that a person who can't read can't be free, I teach. I teach because I dream of a world in which all are free, free to name the world, and free to name themselves and to hear the names of others.

A middle-aged person should blush to speak those words. I wrote them once, I should be ashamed. What does it mean in terms of my classroom to change the world? We learn to be fondly indulgent of our earlier extravagances, smug about our adjustment to a reality that seems to change us more than we change it. When we turn to talk of practical problems in teaching, to talk of teaching practice, we turn away in embarrassment from all that was noble in our younger selves. Because we tend to think of the practical in connection with the world of production and consumption, of technique and control, of the world as it appears to be to those in power, we disclaim the worlds we meant to make. I blush to read those words I wrote in 1985. But I do not do so because I no longer want to change the world. Nor am I sheepish because I have adjusted to "reality" and no longer believe in the possibility. It's just that we are not used to saying such things in public after a certain point in our lives. The old body thinks it better taste to cover its nakedness.

What would it mean to change the world? How would one embark on such a project? We do so, I said before, by changing students' souls, if I was not too metaphysical for my own taste. Still I think the soul is a useful metaphor. *What* our students learn from us becomes part of the reality they inhabit. *How* we teach—our own attitudes to knowledge, to students, the ambience of our classrooms—is our mode of being in our classrooms. Insofar as our students negotiate and share the classroom world with us, they acquiesce to our ways of being. Looked at in this way, as I have said, the practical questions of teaching become moral questions.

To deal with practical questions, we must develop the capacity for the exercise of practical wisdom. It is the office of education to develop that capacity. Practical wisdom is the pursuit of the highest potential of human culture through action grounded in and bodying forth objects of reflection and contemplation. Through reflection and contemplation we come to know ourselves as creatures with a claim on the world, a stake in it, and to know the world through its claims on us, claims demanding committed action. The difficulty we face is that of identifying the highest potential of human culture and choosing our objects of reflection and contemplation. As great harm can be and has been done by those who think they know what the best of humanness is as by those who would reduce education to skill development and vocational preparation.

Practical wisdom involves two things: the knowledge that we

are implicated in the world *as it is,* that we are implicated in what we know and teach, and open-mindedness. Open-mindedness requires of us more, however, than simply the assertion, "everyone's entitled to his own opinion." That assertion is more likely to betray a close-minded consciousness than anything else—after all it's just someone's opinion. That assertion is both an expression of relativism and the ground of domination. "Everyone's entitled to his own opinion," means that the speaker has stopped listening. He has his own opinion too. When we allow that everyone's own opinion is legitimate, we disown, moreover, the material importance of our own. To have an open mind is to confront, willingly and authentically, the other's story, to enter the story as a dialogue. Open-minded persons *claim* their own knowledge and tell their own stories, but they are always mindful of the fact that they may change their minds. Open-minded persons do not merely tolerate other voices; they listen and respond.

In talking about teaching and in teaching about teaching, it will not do simply to distinguish the skills and activities of teaching, although sometimes it is useful to do so. We must be willing to talk about good teaching and bad teaching. Good teaching enlarges the imagination, bad teaching constricts it. Education is not about what is. Education is about what is not yet but can be imagined. Through failure of imagination people become vicious. One thinks of Hannah Arendt's exploration of the banality of evil. How does one teach another—a future teacher—such things. Unless the student somehow, however inchoately, already knows them and shares the ambition to change the world, it can seem like trying to teach a pig to sing. It wastes your time and annoys the pig. The reader (you and I) is struck by the way what I have said so far silences rather than invites dialogue.

I began this essay after the following incident which occurred about ten weeks into the semester the first time that I taught my seminar in curriculum and teaching. A student, unable any longer to suppress his exasperation, burst out, "I still don't see what all the fuss is about—all you have to do is go in and tell kids some things, and then they know them too. That's all you've been doing—talking." Silence. The other students in the seminar try to make themselves invisible. Nothing happens for what seems a very long time while night presses up against the window. The snow hits the glass with its distinctive November sharpness.

Finally I managed to say, "Kevin, haven't you heard a word I've been saying? I've just spent ten weeks talking about why that's not true." To which the indomitable and very certain Kevin replied, "Oh, I heard you all right; I just don't believe you." Does there come a time when you admit that you're trying to teach a pig to sing? Does a teacher have any business to admit such a thought? It is hardly an open-minded one.

Kevin was right about something so obvious about teaching, that we never notice it, something so obvious and so important. There it is, the purloined letter, and here we are, rushing about turning out the drawers of our consciousnesses examining the problems of teaching.

When we teach we talk. Language is our medium of exchange, but it seems that our words have little cash value. Kevin did not say, "I don't believe what you say." He said, "I don't believe you." Our discussions of justice, freedom, empathy, commitment, and care may help to pass the time; they may even be diverting, but they are attached neither to objects nor experiences.

We do not expect truth in this age. For truth we have plausibility and exigency. We have lived through nearly two decades distinguished by lies and duplicities of all sorts. We and our students live in a world of public lies. Politicians lie; newspapers lie; advertisements lie; television lies; our teachers lie, telling us, like the sophist Lysias, only what those in power believe to be true. Rather than feel any outrage over this state of affairs, though, we congratulate ourselves for learning to see through the trick. We become cynical. The trick is to reproduce the lie, something students are very good at, as are we ourselves.

There is a great deal said and written these days about the difficulty of "getting" teachers (Them) to use research results. One gets the sense that teachers are for some reason less skilled in deriving practical implications from theory and research than we are. Of if they are not, institutional factors prevent their employing the skills and knowledge they have acquired in their preparation programs and in-service workshops. I am suggesting an alternative. Perhaps they don't believe us. Perhaps those who seem to profit from our wisdom and instruction are the most consummate liars. Kevin did not say, "I don't believe what you say," because no one expects me to be telling the truth. What I say is play currency in the game of classroom exchange. Someone who does not believe what I say can be persuaded if we simply refer him to the rules of the game. Kevin, who does not believe *me*, has taken his hat off the board and gone home to watch TV.

What about those students who remain in the game? They compete eagerly for Park Place. Still they're not about to have their monthly checks from home sent there. These are the students who say the right things, who make me happy, who know just what I'm looking for when I read their stories. Suspecting this brings me no nearer to achieving my desire. I want them to reconnect their words to things and actions, own their own stories, their names for the world, speak in their own voices. I know that I want the same for myself.

My students are, for the most part, academically successful. They have attended first-rate secondary schools and acquired the necessary skills there. They have also acquired some facility in the language of independence, freedom, and democracy. They have heard about "critical thinking" and try to engage in it as often as they can. Isn't that what I'm looking for after all? But these same students confronted with the facts of unequal distribution of life-maintaining resources and with world starvation, say that while it is unfortunate, that's how things age. These are badly educated human beings. To the extent that we are educated, we will be made uncomfortable and moved to action in the face of human misery and brutality. To the extent that we are educated we will be able to imagine a world free of misery, slavery, and injustice. But this can happen only if such words as "independent thinking," "critical intelligence," "open-mindedness," "tolerance," "democratic participation," etc. are reconnected to human experience, when they are uttered as expressions of our commitments. To the extent that we are educators, our work involves the freeing of the imagination so that words can be fastened to reality. This project demands rather more than giving information, about either theory or practice. It demands that we live our words and work with the other toward a common language. I don't believe you. We do not share a common language. What I must be claiming here, of course, is that speaking in their own voices requires that they speak my language, that their names for the world should flow comfortably from my tongue. This is one of the ironies of teaching for freedom, and the source of many ethical dilemmas.

Some will object that I make too much of the disgruntled

student's chance remark. Why not dismiss Kevin as one of those who proudly holds his naive and common-sensical disdain for "mere theory." Kevin himself would no doubt repudiate the story I've just told. I don't believe you. We cannot talk.

My story is a convenient fiction, a practical fiction, we might say. A practical fiction is an enabling construction, a metaphor for the reality it then constructs. It is an assertion of faith, or if you prefer, domain assumption, paradigmatic proposition, principle, or framework assumption. It is a story in which I, as central character, control the narration. I am no Polonius, "here to swell a scene or two." I tell my story. A practical fiction is an inscription, through my practice, of my reading of the world. It is a narration of my reading which in the telling constitutes my world of practice. And so I am embarrassed to admit that I want to change the world.

My story about Kevin discloses my need to be understood, and my sense that to be understood is to be believed. It exposes my fear that I will not be believed. This fear is a consequence of the distrust of language and stories that afflicts reader and writer both in "Teaching the Text." This wanting to be known, comprehended and acknowledged is the impulse to works of reason and the imagination, is (and I blush) the impulse to teaching.

When we teach we talk. And our talk amounts to more than giving information. In our talk we seek those who understand us, acknowledge us, share our passions. We seek an audience; we create an audience. We reveal ourselves to find those with whom we can speak. We profess. When I teach I tell the story of my life if only I can. Like the ancient mariner assaulting wedding guests, I have no alternative. I don't believe you.

The texts we teach are narratives furnished by others with spaces left for us to accent with our own resonances, inflections, and intentions. Our narratives, our inscriptions of these texts, become for our students workrooms in which they speak the stuff of our texts with their own resonances, inflections, and intentions to produce an original relationship with the stories. I look through a text and I find teaching and learning everywhere. Here it is in Ralph Waldo Emerson's idealism:

> . . . Each age it is found, must write its own books. They [books] are for nothing but to inspire. I had better never see a book than to

be warped by its attraction clean out of my orbit, and made a
satellite instead of a system. The one thing in the world of value, is
the active soul. This every man is entitled to . . . Man thinking
must not be subdued by his instruments. . . . We hear that we may
speak. . . . One must be an inventor to read . . . [then] every page
of every book we read becomes luminous with manifold illusion.[62]

We hear that we may speak. In speaking the world it becomes
my story. I have control over my fate. I am a major character in the
world of my story rather than the subject of some omniscient and
transparent narrator. I become so by imagining possibilities which
I act on.

Shoshona Felman uses psychoanalytic theory to understand
teaching. Psychoanalytic theory is erected on stories; its method is
storytelling. Freedom is found in narration. According to Felman,
teaching, like psychoanalysis, is a struggle against ignorance.
Ignorance is not an absence of knowledge. It is not an empty space
waiting to be filled by information. Ignorance is an expression of
resistance to the knowledge which subjects already have in their
possession.[63] This seems true to me. Not true; it has the ring of
truthfulness.

I don't believe you. I say this, reading a student journal, a
journal written by a student who has figured out quite clearly
what I'm looking for. I don't believe you, your story does not ring
true. You talk abstractly about subjectivity, relation, caring,
democracy, cultural reproduction. You don't know what it means.
You're smug. I'm angry. It means nothing to you. Your language
is corrupt. Emerson said that it is the business of wisdom to attach
words to visible things.

When we teach we talk. We must make our project that of
fastening our words to visible things. Our talk is a text woven
from the strands of our political and intellectual commitments;
each strand added makes a new text. The personal informs the
text, while the text provides access to the personal. In fastening
words to reality, we connect the intellectual and the personal; we
construct a conversational bridge between the public and the
private, the self and the community. Our success in this project
depends upon our willingness to give ourselves up to other voices
even as we move away from them. This is open-mindedness—
neither submissive nor resistant, neither relative nor absolute.
(How curious that can have written this in the register of
resistance as I once did.)

When I read students' autobiographical writings and their journals, I find the stock heroes of American popular culture. I find it difficult to believe that so many students from the socioeconomic background of those attending this university were members of their high schools' oppositional culture. I don't believe the young woman with the outrageous purple earrings and the luminous fingernails when she writes that appearance is unimportant to her. Like all of our famous models and television stars, she just throws on any old thing in the morning. She knows what I'm looking for. She tells me next that she will have to guard against her distaste for high schools girls who seem to think of nothing but appearance. I don't believe the student who has always wanted to teach because she loves kids and is good with them. When I observe her teaching, she has not yet learned the names of her fifteen seventh graders. I don't believe that any of my students hold the contempt they claim for authority— Authority, yes, the school superintendent, no. I don't believe the voice of common sense when it tells me that it's wrong to be a friend to your students. Nor am I sympathetic to the one who wants to be a friend. I don't even know what you mean. I don't believe that it's all subjective—whatever it is. Nor do I believe that grammar is objective and hence boring. And I don't believe that talking about ourselves is, in itself, worth very much.

I cannot say any of this. People must learn for themselves to recognize a counterfeit. I have no doubt that if I were to say, "Your words must be attached to visible things," I would receive pages and pages of "fresh" description.

When we talk about education, we talk about a public phenomenon. We talk about the production, confirmation, and distribution of knowledge in the interest of some public good. But when we talk about teaching and learning, we talk about private phenomena as well. The practice of teaching demands that we understand the way in which the private and the particular instantiate the public and the general, and the way in which the public and the general inform the private and particular. Practical wisdom in teaching is the disposition to transform knowledge into experience and experience into knowledge by acknowledging relationship and connection. The person so disposed has distance from the personal and a radical, personal nearness to the public.

Perhaps women writers have always known this. I think of Charlotte Brontë's *Jane Eyre* whose pilgrimage to self-identity must be negotiated within the limits of sociability, whose journey leads her to the knowledge that abstract principle and law may sometimes conflict with her own nature, who must learn to take the necessary risks to be able to tell her story. I think of the fact that Jane's story is autobiography while her progenitor writes under a man's name.[64]

It has been said that it is the office of literature to test the relationship between language and reality. It has also been said that literature must be judged according to its truthfulness and care. A story should ring true. We may not be able to specify in advance what a story that rings true is like, but we know one when we hear it. When we teach we talk.

Those of us who have been committed to the emancipatory potential of education, who have tried to subvert the authoritarian and hierarchical institutions in which we and our students work, have encouraged some form or other of storytelling. Most commonly, these stories are journals. The problem with journals written for this purpose is that the writer usually tries to hide. No doubt for good reason. At bottom, I suppose, we do not trust each other. We do not trust ourselves.

Stories may be more truthful than reports. Stories can be shared in a way that journals cannot. They draw us into a common world. Our readings tell us what is shared. Stories can be criticized as journals cannot.

I have talked already about the content of the stories I ask my students to write. Now I want to repeat some of these stories as illustrations of practical fictions or as failures.

I once observed a student introducing a poetry unit to her ninth grade class. It was unlikely that any of these students had been exposed to serious poetry before. Their teacher began by introducing the concept of scansion. She then projected on the wall fragments of difficult poems and scanned them. She never read an entire poem. She had apparently forgotten everything she had learned about the difference between the logic of a subject and naive readers. She had forgotten about the importance of student motivation and interest and of the necessity for her to organize and find a point of entry for her students.

She was as aware as the rest of us of the seconds creeping past each other toward the lunch break an eternity away. I asked her why she had done what she had done. She said that that's the way she had been taught poetry—in her college poetry writing seminar. She knew the lesson had failed. I asked her why she had enrolled in that seminar. She said because she already loved poetry, because she had been writing poetry for years. She had begun writing love poems in the tenth grade. A familiar story. We're comfortable with it. I asked her to write the story. I asked her to write another story also, one in which she would be a student in the class she had just taught, suffering this introduction to poetry.

In her story she got inside the itching skin of the boy squirming in his chair in the second row. She saw that what she taught was impenetrable. With her imagined student she became impervious to the poems for all of the teacher's keen penetration of them. She knew the teacher was boring, and poetry was an eternity of perplexity. Her story rang true. It recalled her to herself and to poetry. She was then able to salvage her poetry unit.

The field of curriculum and teaching has often been criticized for being ahistorical and atheoretical. We have been urged to consider the theory-boundedness of all experience and all perception. Some have responded to this call by retreating from the world at once. They are theory blinded. I teach because I want to change the world. I teach because I believe that those who have known their lives to be figured in the lives of others through art and literature and science will acknowledge the claims of others.

When we teach we talk. But we also do other things. We read and we listen. Our reading and our listening are as revealing as our talking. While the author certainly wants to be comprehended by a reader, that reader has a wide latitude within which to construct the writing. The work becomes both more and less than itself; it no longer belongs only to the writer. Teaching is different in this way. The author of a book living in Los Angeles is unlikely to be disturbed by my readings of—or perhaps my distortions of—his point of view. Were we to try to do something together with that book, though, things would be different. We would need a common place; we would need to understand the relationship between his intention and my interpretation. We should need to see them as the occasion for each other. Our conversation about the work would become another work. In that conversation we would meet. In that conversation we would learn the ways that text and interpretation figure one another. In our conversation we would make a common language. When I teach I seek a common language.

In my initial construction of the notion of a practical fiction, I was blinded by theory. I was blinded by all of those literary, epistemological, and ethical theories that assured me that I could arrive at stable, defensible (teachable) conclusions regarding texts even as I acknowledged the radical existential freedom of others to make those texts. In the essay of which this chapter is a revision, I included two specimen stories, one good one (it rang true) and the other untruthful. I talked about ways of criticizing these pieces as if I were a reader with immaculate perception. I now read myself into these stories.

As one begins to read oneself into the stories, the shadows of ourselves take on substance. In the earlier version of this chapter I was impatient with a student's self-aggrandizing. Her story was one of a magnificent lesson, one that had the truants and detention room regulars riveted. They were bad boys only because they were bored. Their new young teacher was different. They loved her.

The story I praised brought us into a classroom where *A Farewell to Arms* was being taught. The story was a story of subtexts in which each member of the class tells a story in a voice that mingles with the voices of the other storytellers. The novel being taught becomes a pretext for students' stories to emerge, sometimes in resistance to the work, sometimes in resonance, sometimes in negotiation. The first story is, of course, a version of "I teach because I want to change the world."

We often remark that all intellectual work is finally autobiographical. We believe that we can learn a great deal about people by attending to the themes and problems which inform their work. Professor X, who has never been certain of anything in his life, not even about what he should have for lunch, spends his whole life refining methods and adducing criteria according to which we may attain certain knowledge about things. Lonely old Professor W devotes his life to research on friendship. Often we are the last to understand the relationship of our work to our lives.

From my own fiction, my story of my encounter with Kevin, I learn something about my work and my life. While it is by no means obvious that my exchange with Kevin is a minidrama displaying the essential horror at the root of skepticism, it is also no accident that I interpret it as such. I share with Professor X a craving for certainty. Nor is it an accident that in the two stories, I preferred the tentative and complex to the cheerful and straightforward one. Not coincidentally either, I preferred cleverness in form and language to uncomplicated dream making.

We teach texts. In the scene of interpretation, our teaching is also a text—a text of selected and anchored meanings that should be the occasion for but not the conclusion of our conversation with our students. When we teach we talk. But when we teach, we speak that we may hear.

I no longer criticize students' stories in the old way. Nor do I ask them to. Instead they now teach their stories providing the rest of us with a pretext for exploring our responses to more general problems in teaching. We read to discover ourselves figured in the stories and in the language of our colleagues. Each of us asks what speaks to us personally in the work, what we sympathize with, what we are uncomfortable with. We find ourselves in conversation with the author and explore what we already know that permits this conversation.

In "A Chair Is A Terrible Thing To Waste," the author wrote a story based on a remark that one of her tenth graders had made: "The teachers here think they own us! They treat us like furniture or something." The story is set in "Hometown High School." The students (like those this author was teaching) spend most of their time in school fantasizing about the real life that will begin when they can leave school at sixteen. Their revenge on their teachers for their imprisonment was obdurate and insistent ignorance. They took great pleasure in nicknaming their teachers. The French teacher was known as Mr. Chaise-Longue, and Mr. Boyd as Mr. Lay-Z-Boyd, for example. In the face of all of this, the teachers remained diligent and committed to education. One day one of the worst kids, while rocking back and forth in his chair tipped right over backwards, and then

> . . . a deep purple spot began to grow on his head. When it got to be about the size of a quarter, a laser beam shot out from its center and the chair was shrouded in an orange mist. The beam was steady for thirty seconds, then disappeared in a flash of purple light.

The boy's mind, all unknown to him, had been enjoying school right along. It had taken this opportunity to escape the tormenting body and take up residence in the chair. The now talking chair made an impassioned speech. It said that since the students loafed around like objects, a mind would do just as well in a chair as in a human body. From that day forward, the shaken students eagerly pursued their studies while the chair went on to become mayor of an administration dedicated to the pursuit of academic excellence.

The author of this story had reported the tenth grader's remark after the first week of her student teaching experience. She was on his side, indignant on behalf of all students whose teachers treat them like furniture. She wrote the story after eleven weeks of teaching. The author is a teacher who wants to make the world a better place, whose sympathies are with the disenfranchised and the silenced. She wants to teach because she believes that the study of literature is, or should be, empowering. She is like most of my students.

I read in this story an anger and frustration that I recognize from my own history. I chuckle with the students when they call the school psychologist, Mr. Barstool. I laugh when the laser beam appears. To me this story is about power and responsibility and faith and rejection. In our group discussion, with the author acting as teacher, we talk about feelings we've had of working very hard for no return. We talk about why we continue to do so. We talk about powerlessness. Nothing can help but a bolt from the blue or a laser beam. We talk about the fantasy that what we do makes a difference even if it does not appear to. Finally we talk about the anger and self-doubt that lead us to accuse our students of willed stupidity.

"Where Love and Need Are One," begins as follows:

> So much depends on our expectations. What Dominick expected
> from teaching was nothing short of salvation. But salvation was not
> on his mind this Friday morning as he fumbled around with a
> fourth attempt at getting his tie right. "Damn! I'm out of practice,"
> he mumbled. The truth was he had never been in practice. This
> time the narrow end wound up shorter than the wide end and the
> tie didn't hang below his belt. "At last." He pulled the knot tight,
> folded his collar down and straightened up to look in the mirror on
> the entry coatrack. "Annie are you sure this coat goes with these
> pants?"

The first part of the story recounts Dominick's reflections on his past life, his current ambitions, and his student teaching situation. He feels good about things, optimistic about his future and the decisions he's made, proud of the successes he's already had in teaching. Many of these reflections he shares with his wife. He is a good teacher and a loving one, one committed to acknowledging his students and to thinking about what it means to do so.

The central incident of the story occurs in a twelfth grade writing workshop. The assignment for the day is "Remembering People." Students read their pieces aloud to their classmates, each of whom responds first by saying what he or she likes about the piece and then by making recommendations for strengthening it. A student who was to read that day approached the author before class to talk about her writing. It was about her boyfriend who is African American. She is caucasian. This is a rural school. Other students, particularly males, had been giving her a bad time, as had her parents. She wrote to affirm her belief in the rightness of her choice. When it was over she cried. Her best friend hugged her, and she cried. Some of the males muttered racist remarks.

The author's turn to comment came around. He had been concentrating on willing order, hoping not to have to deal with anything overtly ugly. He chose to criticize the paper because it had concentrated on describing a relationship and its problems rather than on describing a character. This is the old "Very-nice-but-you-haven't-done-the-assignment" dodge. Open hostilities were avoided, and the class went on as usual.

The author's relief is short-lived. His cooperating teacher observes that the student displayed a great deal of courage in writing and reading her paper. He says, "I think I might have told her so." In the parking lot, the author meets two of the male students. They had just driven her to the dentist's office to tell her how brave she was. At the end of the story:

> Dominick wandered wearily towards his car. His shoulders slumped, he stared at the wet macadam. Unconsciously, rhythmically he opened and closed his left fist; two fingers of his right hand methodically rubbed at his brow. A cold ball of guilt rose in his stomach. Where had he been? Everyone had seen it but him. He was aware of the cold wet penetrating his clothes. "But then," he thought, "what did I expect?"

The question of teacher expectation is one we are accustomed to addressing in terms of teachers' expectations of students. In this story we examine our expectations of ourselves. We ask what is it that we want—for ourselves. Our discussion of this story led us through our own expectations to Dominick's guilt. Why did he respond by feeling guilty rather than, say, disappointed? Why did the other characters' admiration of the young woman's courage leave him feeling disgusted with himself? These questions about the story took us back to power. In our preoccupation with our own needs, in this case the need to be a good teacher, we can fail to listen. In looking at the unresolved tension between Dominick and his wife at the beginning of the story and relating it to his guilt at the end, we understood Dominick's guilt over neglecting his wife and we wondered if that had not made him so preoccupied with running his class smoothly that he forgot to listen. Some of us wondered about guilt as Dominick's dominant mode of response. We speak that we may listen.

"The Apprentice" is also a story about expectation, blindness, and identity. We meet the central character, Julie Gray, while she is dressing on the first day of her student teaching semester:

> She arrived at the last stage of her routine, her hair, and found herself facing her fear of the day again (remember Dominick's tie); but this time with less uncertainty. She knew what a teacher looked like; she'd had millions of them. She pulled her hair back from her face and tied it in a knot at the base of her neck. "This is what a teacher looks like," she noted, satisfied with the result. She had contemplated purchasing glasses even though her eyesight was fine, but had finally decided against it. She would find some other device over which to peer at the urchins. She had been a student long enough now to know what teaching was all about. She scurried out the back door and began her 1/4 mile walk to the high school: nerves a mess, but bun in place, she began her first day.

The teacher in this story is convinced that learning occurs only when students are active, and she believes that her students are more important than her subject. She wants them to be comfortable in her class and to feel good about themselves and each other. This story is the tale of a misconceived assignment.

After reading "The Celebrated Jumping Frog of Calaveras County" to the class, a story which they like well enough, their teacher asked them to write a tall tale using odd language and exaggeration to create humor. The assignment was received with confusion, anger, and cries of, "That's not fair." The teacher was bewildered. She was also annoyed. Later in the day she overheard one of the girls in her class tell a friend that she hated the student teacher. She hates the teacher, she says, because she is unfair and gives impossible assignments. The teacher is hurt. But as she begins to think about the assignment and the student's anger, she begins to learn that our conscientious attention to our models and beliefs can deflect our attention from our students. At that point

> . . . Julie had become the apprentice, the student. The next day she was different. Unconsciously she had changed her appearance. Consciously she had changed her attitude. They would learn now. Yes, they would all learn.

Again the body makes its presence known and again attention is the focus. The student teacher seems to be two persons—Miss Gray, the teacher, and Julie, the student. We talked about the ways in which our entry into institutions seems to require an institutional identity, a masquerade almost. We talked again about relationship and about theoretical abstraction. We talked about desire, the teacher's desire.

In "An Ordinary Occurrence" the student teacher witnesses a teacher's abuse of a second grade child. She is in a room correcting papers with her cooperating teacher. In a room across the hall, she hears

> Brian! Get up here! Well, Mr. Hot Shot, how did you get to be so smart? Maybe you'd like to teach my class? What? What was that? You know, Brian, I've had just about enough of your antics. If you think that your other teachers and I aren't on to your little game—well, you've got another think coming young man. What? Speak up! What did you say? Brian, look at me! I said, look at me! Now stand up straight and tell everybody what you just said. Go on, what's the matter, lost all your nerve? I thought you wanted my attention? No? You wanted it, all right, but on your own terms. Well, that's not the way it works around here buddy. I call the shots around here, and don't you forget it.

At first the student teacher thought it must be some joke. When she realized that it was not, she waited for her cooperating teacher to respond in some way; she hoped that he, or failing that, someone else, would intervene and put a stop to it. Finally, she got up and closed her door on the horror show. Still she waited for her supervisor to say something. He was silent.

In the cafeteria, Brian was being yelled at for being late to lunch. He was late because his teacher had been yelling at him. Meanwhile, other teachers in the cafeteria were talking admiringly about Brian's teacher's toughness. "We can always count on Mary to iron out the problem kids for us." As Mary herself said, "You've got to be tough if you don't want to be jerked around!" The student teacher wanted to interrupt; she wanted to say that it was wrong to speak to any child like that. Instead she tried to look preoccupied with her lunch.

We were all ashamed for our own failures to act when we should have. And we all wondered what it is about institutional roles in the drama of the classroom that would permit one person to talk to any other person in that way.

While our readings do not necessarily agree, our discussions of them enlarge the scene of interpretation. The story helps us. It helps us because we know more than we can say, and the story shows us that in what it does not say. The story reveals more than its language and connects us both to language and to what it means. The story has brought me to be aware that simply trying to say what we mean and mean what we say is inadequate.

In telling and reading stories, we become aware of the unconscious fears and motivations which separate us from our intentions. In fictionalizing our work together in this way we help each other to imagine possibilities. Like the story, theory involves more than we can say, implicates us beyond its language. Authority now becomes a question of authorship. Authorship is warranted not by truth, but by truthfulness. Truthfulness can be judged only in a common language. A language is common when it can mean more than we can say because we have the knowledge of connectedness that the story asserts.

6

Teaching Women

Teaching is an art form. It is also something more than an art form, demanding a perspective on itself and its audience that the artist need not have. I shall not argue for that claim since there can be no disagreement if you accept certain paradigmatic propositions, as Wittgenstein called them, and there can be no argument if you do not. A teacher's medium is the narrative; narratives enact our connection to our work and to each other.

When we teach we tell stories. We tell stories about our disciplines, about the place of these disciplines in the structure of human knowledge. We tell stories about knowledge, about what it is to be a human knower, about how knowledge is made, claimed, and legitimated. The stories that we tell are stories built on other stories; they forge continuity between our stories and those of others, to confirm community among ourselves and others, and to initiate others into our communities. That stories are performances as well as tellings is important. They express *and* represent.

In educational theory we tell stories of teaching, stories that at once reveal, constitute, and confirm the values giving significance to pedagogical acts, to that which we enact in our classrooms. At the theoretical level the story is more concerned with representation, although, as we shall see, it cannot be wholly assimilated to its representational function. These are stories in which we represent those whom we teach in their relationship to ourselves and in which we define the nuances of the relationship, identity, power, and authority of individuals in their relationship to a community and its knowledge.

I am interested in those stories of teaching that tell us its practice is an art and that the curriculum is an art form. I am interested in the languages of those arts and of women's position in them. Finally, I am interested in stories about women as teachers, hence in stories about the relationship between women and art and between women and the practice of the art of teaching. In particular, I am interested in the art of women teaching women.

The business of women teaching has always been thought problematic. Henry Barnard is not the only one among our nineteenth-century fathers to have concerned himself with the injurious effects of hard intellectual work on women's fragile psyches and with the yet more deleterious effect on their precious wombs. But the continuing problem of women teachers is authority. During the nineteenth century one of the chief arguments against women's teaching in the secondary schools was their small size and fragile emotionality. Common wisdom was that they would be unable to control the "big boys." The business of education is something like a football skirmish, and the exercise of authority amounts to subduing the other's body.

The business of authority and in what it consists, who can legitimately exercise it, whether it is possible for a female teacher to exercise or be an authority, continues to figure as a prominent theme in discussions of women teaching. It recurs with some frequency in feminist writing as women struggle to devise nonauthoritarian ways of teaching. The apparent contradictions between such activities as testing, evaluating, grading, and syllabus control and the nurturing and empowering aims of feminist pedagogy are regularly adduced as issues of authority and its vicissitudes. Other have written about the ways in which women teachers are disdained by their students: if they adopt the postures and attitudes of their male colleagues, they are feminist bitches and trying too hard; if they attempt to teach from a nonauthoritarian feminist position, they are lightweight.[65] Either of these student perceptions undermines the teacher's sense of her own authority. But in contemporary mainstream writing on problems of teaching, issues of authority are conceived within the bounds of management and control and are read as gender neutral. Those stories do not serve us well either. Authority may be one of the most recalcitrant problems facing a feminist teacher. This may be so because all of the tales we know about authority line up under either the heading of domination or of collapse into sentimentality. Feminist pedagogy requires of us new performances and new strategies for narrating those performances.

"Authority" in all of its meanings refers to some sort of power or right. When teaching is considered to be an enactment of a narrative, "authority" refers to the power to represent reality, to signify, and to command compliance with one's acts of signification. Even in this context, though, authority eludes women, or at least makes us uncomfortable. Reading feminist philosophy and literary criticism leads us to suspect that our discomfort may have something to do with women's peculiar relationship to language and to art. Women's powers or rights to represent reality are rights secured to surrogates. By proxy only have we the right to command, to enforce obedience to the father's law. Still, it is doubtful that we ever do it well. Part of the reason is that women are either not represented in the Father's law or are represented as lack or deficiency.[66]

The question of authority is complicated for women when we relate "authority" to "author." In the *Oxford English Dictionary*, the first definition of "author" has to do with making something grow or with the person who originates or gives existence to something. One might presume then that an author would be a mother. But according to the *OED*, the author turns out to be the father who begets. Our author is an artist, a father who begets. An author represents. Art represents. Teaching and art may be seen as cognate activities in that both are acts of representation. To become a human who knows is to become one who knows the world through a language in which the author, he who holds the power (the authority) to represent, is a father. Just as women's relationship to authority in the social world has always been perplexing, so has the relationship of women to language and to writing and to art. This is a topic on which the literature on the art of teaching is silent, either because it has never occurred to the writers on that topic that it matters or because, if called on it, such writers would likely deny that gender ought to make a difference. The truly talented, the story goes, never think of themselves as "women artists" or "women teachers." Women believe and tell this story too. This story has serious consequences for women teaching and for all of us, men and women, teaching women.

If we choose to consider teaching an art, then we must understand it to be a gendered art. Even if women are treated elsewhere in educational discourse, when the discussion turns to the art of teaching, women largely vanish. That Charlotte Brontë did not write Thomas Hardy's novels nor Thomas Hardy Charlotte Brontë's has as much to do with gender as with anything else. And so, too, with our teaching of either Brontë or Hardy. The "oversight" is curious but not mysterious.

I will argue in this chapter that the educational stories we tell and our readings of those stories are, among other things, gendered, even when they appear to be universal and gender neutral. If stories about education are gendered, then our interpretations and criticisms of those stories must also be gendered. As Jonathan Culler argues, texts, or our experiences of texts, change substantially when women read as women— something women have not done until recently. What does it mean to read as a woman?

Feminist theory in education provides us with numerous examples of what it means to read as a woman. Feminist studies of teaching have helped us attune our ears to the conversations and the subtexts murmuring under the foregrounded texts. These studies have enlarged the space of pedagogical discourse and insisted on the gendered nature of pedagogical experience. Nel Noddings, for example, has brought us to an awareness of the liberatory and humane possibilities of an education which honors a feminist ethic, a plural rather than a singular ethic, one of love rather than of duty.[67] Like Carol Gilligan she has tried to rescue morality from the abstract and to situate moral discourse in the realm of personal relations. Jane Roland Martin, in entering the conversation of educational theory, has made us take women seriously, not as surrogate men, but as gendered creatures owning a specific genderized knowledge. She has raised the level of the conversation and has made untenable any universal appeal of the Peters ideal or the Hirst model of liberal education.[68] In Madeleine Grumet's work the maternal subtext which is the background of women's teaching is explicitly rendered.[69] All of this work has required that we take women students and ourselves seriously in a way that we have not done before. When educational discourse is enlarged to include women, then what we choose to observe, the stories that we tell, and the principles which guide our action, all change significantly.

A Story

Somewhere I read (I have it written down in a notebook), "Man is a creature of passion who must live out that passion in the world." It was in one of my more undisciplined moments that I wrote that sentence, so I have no idea whose was the fiery mind in which it was forged. Nietzsche's perhaps, or Sartre's. Likely some romantic perched on the end of this thought in one of those moments of soaring far above the quotidian mercantile concerns and conversations of utilitarians and other Philistines. Perhaps it was Freud in one of his more desolately biological moments.

"Man is a creature of passion who must live out that passion in the world." This sentence begins one of those stories meant to tell us how one ought to live, how one ought to live because one has no choice—one *must* live out one's passion in the world. This story is one of those about being human—one of those about a human artist. We might read this as a description of a world which exists only as an object of passion—of my passion. We might read this sentence equally well as the beginning of one of those stories about knowledge which began to appear during the eighteenth century, as well as about art. Then the tale teller is a skeptic. The source of his passion is another matter. Libido perhaps. Libido transformed, but libido nonetheless. Or perhaps the sentence begins a story of failure, a tale of the failure of human knowledge to constitute a meaningful life. The tale may be intended as a charm to protect the teller from despair over the inadequacies of human knowledge by making a virtue of necessity. Perhaps the sentence begins one of those compensatory tales of "other-minds skepticism" as Stanley Cavell describes it—the knowledge that we can never know the Other as we know ourselves.[70] We have read some of these stories in preceding chapters.

Of course, the sentence and the creature uttering it may not *begin* a story at all. Perhaps we are at the end. Perhaps we have reached the end, in that sentence, of a spiritual saga that spans the distance from the radical skepticism of Hume to the radical indifference of Nietzsche to the apparent elimination of desire in twentieth-century analytic philosophy. We may simply have found ourselves settled into the old familiar conclusion in postmodern literature:—the story is only about itself but that desire for an object, a subject matter of the story, is unslakeable. In any case, the story in which that sentence is meaningful *is* a story about *man*, about *man's* impulse to art and about *his* relation to knowledge. It is a story deeply embedded in a peculiarly male anxiety. But it is a story we all have heard and learned to repeat in the course of our educations.

As I write, I find myself getting away from myself. The assertion distracts, and yet that creature of passion who has no choice but to live out his passion in the world exerts a fatal fascination. In some ways I know him better than I know myself. Of course, I have had a great deal more experience with him than I have with myself. His is the voice of the great Western bourgeois tradition; his is the voice which sets the pitch for mine. I am his creation; he is the professor of desire. And what does he profess, this secular Jonathan Edwards of a professor? What does he desire? I ask these questions because he has been my teacher. As his student, I strove to satisfy his desire; as a teacher, I have taken his desire for my own. He seduced me no less than did Socrates in inviting me into the scheme of noble loving.

When I was in college I took a course in mythology. I am certain I met my creature of passion many times there. It was taught by a woman in a soft green sweater with a mothhole near the wrist of the right sleeve, the only female teacher I had as an undergraduate, and only one of two in graduate and undergraduate education combined. She wore glasses. On the first day of class she sat on the desk. The rest of the semester, she joined us in a circle. There were only six of us; the red-haired girl was smartest. She always found her way out of the labyrinth first and stood on the magic stones of literature in the brilliant sunlight of definition, waiting for the rest of us to stagger out of the darkness and into language. In our struggle through the maze, we recapitulated the literary project, a project that begins with the birth of the hero and ends with his journey out of the maternal maze, away from his desire for his mother to a state of perfect knowledge and grace. I learned this that year as the standard story of Western civilization. I learned it as timeless and universal. I learned to identify with the hero because, of course, I had been doing so all of my life. I simply had not yet learned to call it "Western civilization." This journey too leads me away from myself, as indeed did "Western civilization" until I began to read its tales from a gendered perspective. Feminist pedagogy and feminist theory help us to break the spell these stories cast, not to reject them, but to enlarge them and to reconnect them to our own experience rather than permitting them to replace our own experience with one wholly alien.

"The art of teaching" is a subject with a venerable history. Scarcely anyone claiming to be educated has been silent on the matter. It is necessarily part of the discussion of the status and future of culture—real culture, that is, not mass culture. As readers move through the books and essays on this subject, they must infer one of three things: the art of teaching women is no different from the art of teaching men; women teaching are not engaged in art; the teaching of women requires little art. All of these are variants on standard stories in Western civilization. This is not to say that the professors have been silent on the education of women. Because we women are particularly charged with the guardianship of culture (though not its production), the education of women has been of especial interest along with the topic of women's teaching. Women do not beget culture; we mind it—both in the sense of tending and in the sense of obeying. The "art of teaching" and the "education of women" seem to be two very different, and unrelated, topics. The education of women is the education of those who are represented, but not of those who represent; it is the education of those who mind, but not of those who create culture.

Gender is one of the fundamental categories according to which we organize our experience of ourselves and others. A prominent theme in women's writing, both as art and about art, is and always has been that gender makes a difference in the production of art. E. Ann Kaplan argues that the art of filmmaking is inseparable from the male scopophiliac impulse—the need to see without being seen, the need to see the maternal body.[71] Virginia Woolf over and over again notes the ways in which a woman's sensibility differs from that of a man. Sandra Gilbert and Susan Gubar explore the images peculiar to the female literary imagination.[72] Feminist literary theorists in general question the standards of literary production and taste. The stories women tell are very different from the stories men tell. Their difference has been sufficient to consign most of these stories to the realm of the sentimental and minor in literary judgment. When these stories are so judged, they are judged to be so against the apparently neutral universal standards imposed by the totalizing tendencies of patriarchal discourse. If they are read instead as presenting vital alternative visions to those which ground patriarchal storytelling, we revise our assessment of them. We see them differently. Feminist rereadings of the domestic literature which was, until recently, dismissed as inconsequential argue that that literature in fact is to be identified with concerns unlike the gentlemanly and heroic concerns which define the canon.[73] Margaret Homans' studies of Dorothy Wordsworth, George Eliot, the Brontë's, Elizabeth Gaskell, and Virginia Woolf, explore the terrain of a peculiarly female imagination traversable only by those who employ a specifically female set of linguistic strategies.[74] If gender makes a difference in art, it must then make a difference in the practice of the art of teaching as well. But the literature on the art of teaching suggests that the teacher is sexless, that artistic teaching is simply artistic teaching and gender neutral. Of course this view is compatible with the dominant conception of the artist in our culture.

In "Where the Line is Drawn," Madeleine Grumet offers us a different vision of the teacher artist.[75] Grumet follows the path from domestic world to public world, from the world of contemplation to that of practice and back again. She asks for the distance demanded by aesthetic practice and for the community that is the condition of its expression. Her vision of artistry is a dialectical one, shuttling between the poles of subjectivity and objectivity, of experience and narration. Her vision refuses participation in the economy of dominance and submission that marks the male artist or the male storyteller in patriarchal culture. Her vision fuses self with other, artist with object while clearly observing and maintaining the line between, however that line may shift as the geography changes.

Artistry demands an attitude, a way of being in the world. The artist in modern Western culture has been precisely that man who is a creature of passion and who must live out that passion in the world, a passion psychoanalytic theory tells us is a passion to possess the absent and unpossessable mother—she-who-is-presumed-to-know, the source of life and the truth of his paternity. *His* passions, and the anxieties associated with them, are very different from those of the woman artist. In his work he transforms the raw stuff of his passion into an image of the world crafted in the likeness of his own beautiful soul. He becomes his own substitute for the absent and forbidden mother. His passion is the foundation of our culture; through it he represents to us the deepest values and anxieties shared by members of our communities. His passion is firmly lodged in the economy of domination and submission. He is the solitary one, the man who stands outside of traditions and social structures. Lonely and disdained, with a sensibility so finely drawn that he must loathe the mess and fuss of everyday life, the talk that neither inspires nor enlightens, he spends himself only in his work—the endless creation and recreation of the woman suitable to protect his genius. Something inevitably goes wrong though, and he makes a shrew or a whore.

Few men are so fortunate as Pygmalion who, Susan Gubar argues, embodies myths of male primacy, myths which enable the male to evade "the humiliation, shared by many men, of acknowledging that it is *he* who is really created out of and from the *female* body. [Gubar claims that] such myths, securing for the male that creative power which makes women fearsome to him, act to limit women's options for self-expression to the medium of their own bodies and faces."[76] What is involved in the art of teaching for such men? What have women to do with such art? When we find ourselves represented, we are either exemplars of virtue or objects of derision and fear. We are either above the world, and so worthy to be its guardians, or we are the source of all evil in the world. Those of us women who would be artists must reject this vision.

Women are the objects out of which art is made. And the art which women have made has often represented just that state. If we cannot become artists, we can, as Gubar asserts, turn ourselves into objects of art. She reminds us of Woolf's Mrs. Ramsey and of Wharton's Lily Bart. Indeed, many have interpreted the situation of the woman in fiction as that of an artist without a medium. Questions of art are pertinent to questions of women's education because what art has made of women, education has made of us. Reading Rachel Brownstein, the female reader is recalled to her own history as a student, as a reader who finds and forms herself in literature. She is recalled to her own experience of the literary heroine as exemplar in her life.[77] Of course we could find ourselves worse heroines than Elizabeth Bennett, the apple of her father's eye, Elizabeth who shares her father's wit and perspicacity, not to mention his good taste in her low opinion of her mother and sisters. Emma Woodhouse, that heroine whom Jane Austen said would be disliked by all but her creator, has her moments.

Jane Eyre is fiercely independent and gets to marry Rochester. But we've seen what happened to Catherine Earnshaw. And what are we to do with Sue Bridehead whose weakness leads to the murder-suicide of her children? The raped and brutalized Tess is there too, and Maggie Tulliver drowned in our dreams with her brother. Thank heaven for Anne Elliott's good sense.

We are affected in our deepest selves by the images and representations of those women in literature and art whom we identify *as women*. We should be shocked and dismayed, then, when we notice that one easily spends four years in college classrooms meeting mostly harlots, courtesans, fishwives, and bourgeois consumers who in the act of consumption consume themselves along with their husbands, children, and best friends. I teach a course, a "core course" at our university, in which we encounter an astonishing number of women for sale or use, along with a violent and threatening Mother Nature who must be brought to her knees and, in the words of one of the scientists in our curriculum, "forced to unveil herself."[78] In a single course, Darwin treats us to a discussion of the passivity of the female of all species and Marx ignores women altogether. *Notes From the Underground* brings us the whore with a heart of gold; Henry Adams introduces us to the American woman who is a failure; he longs for the Virgin; Baudelaire does Baudelaire, and nudes and barmaids and odelisks hang from our walls. So this is Western civilization.

The line is drawn. As Grumet says, in the patriarchal vision we are either exiles in the kitchen or isolated in the bunkers of the sex war. In feminist art, the line is not a barrier. The world enters those rooms of our own, and from these rooms we enter the world of our culture.

Another Story

Teaching women: It's neither an easy thing to do or to be. It is still less easy to talk or write about it when the language of teaching excludes, as it does, women's experience. In *The Small Room* by May Sarton, Harriet Summerson asks Lucy Winters, "Was there ever a life more riddled with self-doubt than that of a female professor?"[79] "No," I said on first reading those words, "there never was. But why did no one ever notice it before?"

Lucy Winters has just taken a position in the English department of a small, elite women's liberal arts college, somewhere—anywhere—in New England. Appleton is every small northeastern liberal arts college, a place of personalities and political conflicts and a place of dedication to a certain notion of educational excellence. The fundamental proposition of the ideology of excellence which defines college life asserts that the price of excellence is exquisite pain and loneliness. The scholar, like the artist, is a solitary figure.

Lucy has just completed a Ph.D. in American literature at Harvard and ended an engagement. She is not sure that she wants to teach, is not sure that she will be a good teacher. In truth, she pursued an advanced degree only in order to be with her fiancé while he was in medical school. Her professional doubts and her personal sadness intertwine. They become equally important to her work as a teacher and in particular, I think, because she is a teacher of young women.

Lucy's story of private failure is precipitated into that of her public commitment and anxiety by her discovery of a case of student plagiarism. The act of plagiarism threatens to ravel the bonds of community so carefully and precariously protected by the fractious faculty which prides itself on its members' distinguishing idiosyncrasies. The student is the favorite of a senior professor, one of a handful of respected scholars in medieval history. Carryl Cope is middle-aged, fiercely brilliant, totally immersed in her work, and dedicated to nurturing genius in those rare cases when it is to be found in a student. She is the professor of desire. Professor Cope has spent four years inspiriting and inspiring Jane Seaman with her own brilliance and ambition. Like Pygmalion molding his wax woman, Professor Cope tried to create a wax student in her own image and tried then to instill in that image her own life and passion. The waxen image she produced was a half-formed and oddly shaped thing, crippled in its spirit, a solitary one, suffering the fire of her brilliance without receiving warmth or comfort. Jane's is a brilliance cracked and dimmed by anger and scorn. Of a paper Jane has written for Lucy's seminar, Lucy says in speaking to her about it:

It was a straight A paper. . . . But I found it disturbing. I'm sure it

gave you great pleasure to tell off so many clever people and prove
yourself, to yourself, a match for them. . . .
You intelligence is, if you will, an angel. You are putting it to poor
work for an angel. Really, that paper was full of hatred and
self-hatred, hatred of the intellect, hatred of all those critics who
can prove themselves superior to the artist they analyse because
they can analyse him.[80]

Jane's anger and scorn congeal in her reading and diffuse
throughout her writing, becoming finally the distinguishing mark
of her identity. Consumed by hatred and self-hatred, she
sabotages that which she believes to be all that legitimates any
claim of hers on the attention or affection of others, in particular
the attention and affection of Carryl Cope—her reputation as a
brilliant student. Without the brilliant heat of her angry
intelligence, what is Jane? How is she to be represented for
others?

Lucy discovers the plagiarism quite by accident as a result of
her rummaging in the library looking for something that might
give her a new slant on teaching *The Iliad* to her first-year students.
Jane Seaman's brilliant analysis of *The Iliad* for a forthcoming issue
of a college journal turned out to have been stolen from "an
obscure and forgotten essay" by Simone Weil. Everything that we
know about living in an academic community demands that Lucy
report her discovery. Like the messenger of Greek tragedy, Lucy's
news sets in motion the machinery of justice and principle, a
machinery which threatens to blow apart the community it was
designed to preserve.

Putting one's own name to another's work may be the gravest
crime known to the academic community. It is interesting that in a
culture in which the appropriation of the labor of others is the rule
rather than the exception, works of the creative mind retain their
claim to individuality and to the right of the producer to control
those works. In a logocentric universe only works of the intellect
seem to give one a claim on the world. In a sense this view
represents a sentimentalization of the life of the mind, a
sentimentalization charted across the degradation of the body.

The English Department at Cornell University distributes to
students (or did in 1982) the following statement on plagiarism:

Since one of the principal aims of a college education is the development of intellectual honesty, it is obvious that plagiarism is a particularly serious offense and the punishment for it is commensurately severe. What a penalized student suffers can never really be known by anyone but himself; what the student who plagiarizes and "gets away with it" suffers is less public and probably less acute, but the corruptness of his act, the disloyalty and baseness it entails, must inevitably leave an ineradicable mark upon him as well as on the institution of which he is privileged to be a member.[81]

Neil Hertz calls this document an extravagant teaching. Analyzing the above statement, he is intrigued by the imagined private consequences speculated on in the statement and by the fact that they are pure fantasy. People do get away with it, and we are probably safe in assuming that some of them do not suffer and that they may in future years have no memory of the act, much less bear an "ineradicable mark." Hertz invites us to imagine the following scenario:

You have either found yourself caught up in the process or listened as some colleague eagerly recited the details of his own involvement. There is first the moment of suspicion, reading along in a student's paper; then the verification of the hunch, the tracking down of the theft, most exhilarating when it involves a search through the library stacks, then the moment of "confrontation" when the accusation is made and it is no longer the student's paper but his face which is read for signs of guilt, moral anguish, contrition, whatever.[82]

According to Hertz, the motivation for this extravagance is a projection, a projection of the professor's anxiety about his own originality stemming from "the self-division implicit in all linguistic activity."·

In words we deceive, and we betray. The anxiety, says Hertz, is "about the kind of 'writing' involved in teaching—the inscription of a culture's heritage on the minds of its young." A student's plagiarizing relieves our anxiety. The fact of institutional violation on the part of another guarantees the integrity between one's own words and one's self, a binding of the self and its signs.[83] "I would never do such a thing. I have never cheated." My words are my own; they are an expression of my life. But where did these come from? Are they really my own? Where do the Other's words come from? What is his life? What is truth? Whom can we trust? This is yet another version of other-minds skepticism and another version of Descartes' doubts.

The binding of self to signs assures a continuity in the stories that maintain our institutions. Our stories are representations of individual identity and of the connection of individuals to communities. The entire network of human relationships is threatened when the word, that representation of identity and emotional bonding, turns out to be false. But these stories, these stories of selves and institutions are male stories signifying the child's successful and distressing separation from his mother. In all cases the child is, however genderless the story makes him appear, a male child still yearning after the story that binds him to the mother. He is trapped in the figures which replace his literal mother, figures which he can trust no more than he can trust the mother.

Man is a creature of passion who must live out that passion in the world. The object of passion, the object of desire, is integrity, integrity in the sense of being undivided, attached—attached to one's life and to one's words. The primal source of this desire for integrity, though, is the infant's powerlessness, his dependence on, his helpless *need* for the often absent and frustrating mother. The mother represents not only frustrated attachment, but a creative power which the child must wrest from her in order to free himself of his need, in order to become individuated and autonomous. The word, the figurative substitute for the absent mother, is under the child's control—in controlling the word, he controls the mother. As the child becomes a man, integrity can be asserted only through the Name-of-the-Father, the Father's word and the Father's law. The irony of this integrity is that it is demonstrated by individualness, by separateness, and, in the academic world, by creative originality that denies its genesis in primal passions. The passionate life of the mind may turn out to have a great deal to do with the mind's displacement of passion onto the cultural heritage and its institutions.

Finally, Appleton's integrity is threatened not by the breaking of the law so much as it is by the recognition of the frightening possibility that the law is inadequate to the task of binding it is charged with. Unlike the messenger in Greek tragedy who is not responsible for his message, Lucy knows that she in fact made a choice, the choice that started the relentless machinery of the law.

She wishes that she had not; she wishes that someone else would take responsibility; she shares none of Hertz's Professor Sherlock's exhilaration. Other members of the community wish that the theft had not been discovered. Somehow, the law of integrity seems, in this case, to require a violation of morality and a violation of all that one thought one was up to in the act of educating. The very definition of education is called into question. Finally, each member of the Appleton community is forced to come face to face with the way in which she is implicated in Jane's act because of the way in which she is implicated in the institution and its laws. Was there ever a life more riddled with self-doubt than that of the female college professor?

Lucy Winters, as riddled with self-doubt as any of us, is a teacher in spite of herself. She has come to Appleton only to escape the world she had inhabited with her fiancé. We learn that he ended the relationship and that his doing so had something to do with their being unable to speak to one another. Lucy describes their difficulty as rooted in the fact that she is a woman and he is a man, that he thinks clearly and rationally, while she thinks sloppily and intuitively. His is a clean world and an ordered one, while hers is a clutter of irrelevant details hanging out of half-closed drawers, a world in which memories and sensations come tumbling out of jammed cupboards. Lucy is not sure that John's way is not superior—a tidy house with a place for everything and everything in its place, a house where one can find one's way blindfolded or blind.

Standing at her office window after having refused a student the emotional response that student was after, Lucy pleads with herself for a world in which all of the irrelevant details and distracting memories and sensations can be neatly pasted into scrapbooks and stacked at the back of the closet shelf. "I want to be free to teach my students in peace," she thought. "I want to be free to do that unself-consciously, without all this personal stuff."[84] And yet she thinks:

> But had one any right to protect oneself? What had she been
> protecting? A relationship that could not be maintained as fruitful if
> it lapsed into personalities? And what was teaching all about
> anyway? If one did not believe one was teaching people how to
> live, how to experience, giving them the means to ripen, then what
> did one believe? Was it knowledge that concerned her primarily?
> And would knowledge alone bring them to appreciate Thoreau?[85]

That education is about teaching people how to live and giving them the means to ripen is in fact exactly what one believes when one talks about the art of teaching. But this is not how art is represented in the patriarchal tradition. Over and over again, the faculty of Appleton speak the same words. They say that teaching is about teaching the person and not just the subject. They say that teaching is an act of dedication. They say that teaching is an art. Jane's act forces us to wonder whether this art can be practiced in the small rooms of professors' offices or in the small room of the life of the mind. What Jane wanted from Professor Cope was the sort of love and approval which confirm her in her Otherness. Jane received books and higher expectations along with the sense that not she, but some power not honestly her own was the basis of her value in the professor's eyes. Just as women are represented but do not represent themselves in the patriarchal tradition, Jane does not exist in herself, in her own voice. She is the object of her professor's desire, a desire which demands that she relinquish her own.

Women students are not unique in wanting something more from us than our passionate intellects lived out in our works of creative genius, our inscriptions of ourselves on the world. The creature of passion who must live out his passion in the world is as unsatisfactory a teacher as he is a lover. Male students are as likely to make the same demands. Women teachers, for whatever reasons, are likely to feel the pull of those demands in ways that their male colleagues do not. At the most obvious level, we need only note that women have a long history of responding to demands for love, for compassion, for nurturance, for *understanding* of the Other. Because we carry with us always our similarity to our mothers, we carry with us always, however inchoately, that first knowledge of connection. The Other is present. At the same time, the knowledge that counts, public knowledge, is mediated by men. We know ourselves and other women primarily in our relationship to men as Virginia Woolf pointed out in *A Room of One's Own*.[86] Feminist theory and feminist pedagogy are attempts to interrupt that mediation. In feminist theory we learn to speak together and to honor the claims of connection and understanding while standing in the middle distance. From rooms of our own, we women come and go, talking no longer of Michelangelo. Was there ever a life so riddled with self-doubt as that of a woman teacher?

Hertz's imaginary professor doubts his own authorship, his own integrity, because he must doubt everything, because his self-inscription, the living out of his passion in the world, inscribes a very specific desire backed by a corresponding fear. Subject-object relations, the very constitution of human subjectivity, and hence the constitution of that which subjectivity intends through its participation in human institutions, flows from patriarchal anxiety. The male's inscriptions in culture and its laws are invocations permitting the inference of paternity and representations of generative control. Language and knowledge in a patriarchal universe are saturated with the unconscious conflicts attending exile from the body of the all-powerful, phallic mother—the one-presumed-to-know. But she is not permitted to know, or at least not permitted to claim her knowledge, for the only available modes of representation are those which insure male creativity, generativity, and legitimacy. The sense of an I and a you emerges at the same moment as does language, as does the power to represent, a power wrested from the maternal gaze.

Psychoanalytic theory teaches us that becoming a woman is an exceedingly difficult psychosexual task.[87] Achieving womanhood—or perhaps more appropriately, a female social identity—requires that we maintain identification with our mothers even as we repudiate our primary love for her. In Homans' language, we turn from the literal body, both hers and our own, in order to enter the world of the figure, the world of the word. Hers is the world that we must leave in order to individuate ourselves from her, even as hers is the world that our futures have in store for us. But because we are like our mothers physically, our turn from the mother to the father is a turning from ourselves. According to Chodorow, a woman's psychic structure is triangular. While in the public world, female relationships are mediated by the male, there persists in the female psychic economy the presence of a third figure who mediates the male-female relationship. The third figure is that of the mother with whom traces of primary identification are retained. Because mothers are women, female experience produces a pre-Oedipal identification with the mother that persists into and beyond the construction of the Oedipal triangle infinitely complicating the female psychic structure.[88] Later in this chapter we shall examine the significance of this complication for women's art and women's teaching.

Social arrangements in the modern West require of the mother

that she deliver both male and female children to the world of the
fathers, to the world of public authority and civic power. But in
that world male and female children are delivered to different
locations. The male child's destination places him in direct
alignment with the structure of authority and power. Although
she enters the world of her brothers and fathers, the female's
situation is problematic in a way that theirs cannot be. For she
carries around inside her the Other whom the laws of the father
require her to relinquish and leave behind—even to repudiate.
The language in which she learns to represent herself and to
maintain in presence the originary human relationship with her
mother is the language of the father, a language which denies the
power of the creative mother. The third in her psychic economy
remains unnamed.

In some ways the relationship of the female teacher to her
students recapitulates the mother-child relationship. Her duty is
to wean the student from dependence on her, from preoccupation
with his or her own subjectivity, to a mastery of the objective rules
of the disciplines and to an independent place in the disciplinary
order. She represents, though, a canon and an institutional text
from which she is excluded, within which she must treat herself as
Other to herself.

Was there ever a creature so riddled with self-doubt as a
female professor? No. There never was. But hers is an anxiety
different both from that of the mother who relinquishes part of
herself and from that of the male teacher. Hers is a compounded
anxiety born of her continued identification with the mother and
her exile in the language and knowledge that is our cultural
heritage inscribed in our father's passions and texts, while yet she
remains the Other of those passions and texts. She is simultaneously the object of art and the surrogate artist who creates,
through the medium of the father's passions and texts, the female
student. The male teacher, like the father, serves directly and
unproblematically as the representative of the abstract world of
order, method, beauty, justice, etc. He is "the reader," "the
scientist," "the philosopher," "the lover," "the artist," the "he"
whose voice we mimic.

Our institutional and disciplinary stories are compensatory, as
Freud taught us in *Civilization and Its Discontents*. They are salve
for the narcissistic wound. But they are male medicine. The
wounds that men and women suffer are different. The male child

loses the Other and the self constituted in the Other's gaze; the female loses both of these things too. But the male child's *difference* permits him, through the process of substitution, to establish a fairly simple dyadic relationship with the mother that will become foundational to all future relationships, epistemological as well as social and political. The shift from pre-Oedipal to Oedipal reality for the male requires that he substitute a like object for the original lost object. Female existence for him becomes a matter of infinite, but fairly simple, substitutions of like objects. His own existence becomes foundational to that of others and of objects in the world. Hence the possibility of Descartes' radical doubt and the intellectual *bildungsroman* which begins with the institution of mind as root and source. Foundations of thought, foundations of knowledge, and disciplinary foundations all have their origins here in this logocentric and polarized universe. One's own knowledge is the measure. The logic of domination begins here.

That shift to Oedipal reality is never complete for the female. Development nonetheless demands of her, too, a total and entire repudiation of pre-Oedipal identification. She must make an erotic shift to the father whose love requires of her complicity in her brother's scorn for the lost object and a final identification with the original lost and repudiated object. The erotic turn to the father retains traces of the pre-Oedipal attachment to the mother. The mother becomes the missing third term completing the female psyche. The feminine erotic is bisexual.

Male art is simple representation, substitution, a reenactment of the original loss attended either by scorn or exaltation of the substituted object. The male psyche is the foundation of art; the world expressed in that art is assimilated to and stands as an analogy for, male need. The world expressed in that art permits our creature of passion to live out that passion in the world. What have women to do with such stories of art or of knowledge? In these stories our silence and our authorial illegitimacy are encoded. Women's art and knowledge begin precisely here, exploring these stories and their subtexts and situating the missing third in them.

Jane's crime is plagiarism. In a way, it is the perfect female crime, much more suitable than poisoning, even when the poison is conveyed to its victim in a lovely red apple. Academic women commonly express the theme of imposture when talking about professional anxieties. Insofar as we speak in our work the language of the exile, are we not all of us plagiarists? We project ourselves into the world through the language that we speak; we obey the conventions of storytelling. But women's inscription is in the character of an inaccessible or despised Other, always beyond reach. Our words speak our lives. Our words replace the original symbiotic wordless connection to the mother, making other connections with other speakers. When women speak, though, we speak in the compensatory language of the fathers, a language that stands in for male separation and male creative anxiety. The language compensates the male for his loss by keeping the mother eternally lost and the woman eternally lost to herself.

Psychologists and other moralists will tell us that Jane's act is a response to pressure. They may tell us that she fears success or that she suffers from a peculiarly female self-defeating personality disorder. Her plagiarism then is read as a cry for the help she cannot ask for, a plea to be caught and punished. But for what crime? Her only crime up until the theft had been academic brilliance. If we are willing to be playful about our most sacred intellectual prejudices, we might argue that in fact Jane's act should be read as a radical reenactment of what it means to be a woman in the academy and as a protest against exile. That she chose to steal an essay by Simone Weil, she whose philosophy is one of radical nearness, of connectedness to its object, is in itself provocative. Simone Weil's work, both in life and in text, contests patriarchal authority. Plagiarism in this case announces connection, a desire to merge with and reestablish attachment to the pre-Oedipal object. At the same time, the subtext of the act for a female may be to reinstitute the lost traces of her own presence, to speak in her own voice. Patriarchal authority is legitimate only because it appeals to something beyond, indeed minimizes the demand for and the threat of intimacy; a philosophy of radical nearness acknowledges both demand and threat.

The question becomes one of possibility. If art and language by their nature exclude women, are born of the male's need for and fear of female otherness, then what can we say regarding a feminist practice, or a feminine practice, of the art of teaching? It would appear to be an impossible achievement.

In "Femininity," Freud announced his discovery of the persistence of pre-Oedipal experience in women's lives. For Freud the pre-Oedipal moment is the "dark continent" of the female psyche, buried as was the Minoan civilization beneath the Cretan and as inaccessible to the hungry eyes of man. The Minoan civilization is a figure for women's pre-Oedipal relationship to their mothers, a relationship that survives the achievement of post-Oedipal heterosexuality. "What do women want?" Freud asked.[89]

Freud hits a note of desperation in that question. As he acknowledges his ignorance of the dynamic of female desire, he recognizes that contrary to his own earlier view, male and female development are not symmetrical. In this moment, female development becomes infinitely complicated. Any understanding of the achievement of femininity resists all attempts to assimilate understanding of the feminine to the masculine dynamic. Man is no longer the measure. All of Freud's narrative ploys and habits of reason fail him at this instant.

The evidentiary base for Freud's theories of human development was literature. Freud himself never got so far as recognizing that that literature was written by men. His self-analysis, his treatment of his patients all devolved on his interpretations of literature and an analysis of present cases that proceeded principally through modes of analogy and assimilation. His reading of the literature that makes up our patriarchal heritage is subtle, perspicacious, and plausible. However, when we consider his one notable failure, his treatment of Dora, we encounter failure of the strategies of analogy and assimilation, recognition of which permeates the later "Femininity."

Dora is often read as a detective story. But it can also be read as a contest for narrative control.[90] It can also be read as a story about the ways in which men passed women around among themselves—Dora's father first handing her over to Herr K. in payment for Herr K.'s indulgence of his wife's affair with Dora's father, and the father's then handing Dora over to the doctor who is to persuade her that there is no affair and that if Herr K. tried to seduce her, she enjoyed it. Although Freud believes Dora's account of events, he denies the authority of her interpretation. Freud takes on the role of the teacher here. His task is to teach the reluctant student to read the deeper thread of her narrative which he read as her repressed attraction for Herr K. and her homosexual desire for his wife. Freud's insistence that Dora's illness masks her sexual desire for her father and is exacerbated by her repressed desire for Herr K. may in fact be read as Freud's story. It is curious that it should never have occurred to Freud that the sexual advances of a forty-six-year-old man would surely be *sexually unwelcome* to a fourteen-year-old girl. Forty is old to fourteen. Old and ugly. But Freud himself was forty-six and himself a sufferer of hysteric disorders. Freud read Dora's transference but not his own, as he later admitted. He also neglected the importance of Dora's mother and what may have been the key to Dora's relationship with Frau K. She says of Frau K.'s children: "I was like a mother to them." According to Freud's own lights, Dora must become like her mother. But Dora's relationship to her mother is ambivalent, so Frau K. stands in for an idealized mother in Dora's negotiation of female identity. And this idealized mother betrayed Dora. Freud had not yet discovered the Minoan civilization, the subtext of Dora's story.

When Freud refuses to permit Dora control of her story, she terminates the analysis, giving him two weeks' notice—"like a governess or a servant," he says. She inverts the master-servant relationship, the male-female relationship. She refuses to play. A year later she returns to Freud for one meeting only to tell him that she has insisted on claiming her knowledge. Against Freud's advice, she has forced her story, the story of her father's affair and Herr K.'s attempted seduction of her, on the adults who have studiously repressed it. Dora's anger wins. Yet Dora is the victim. The knowledge she insists on claiming is the knowledge of her victimization, a knowledge which imprisons her. She marries unhappily and suffers from a variety of psychological and physical complaints until her death. Freud failed as a teacher in this case. He failed because Dora would not and could not take his story as her own. And the pre-Oedipal subtext of her own story remained buried beneath the ruins of patriarchal authority.

Elizabeth Abel's reading of *Mrs. Dalloway* corrects Freud's mistakes with Dora. Using Clarissa Dalloway's development as an example, Abel excavates a Minoan subtext in women's novels. She argues that while courtship or romance plots may dominate the narrative in women's novels, an effort at excavation uncovers a subtext of mother-daughter relations—a subtext "that both predates and coexists with the heterosexual orientation" which appears as the central element of the plot. Development in the female novel, Abel argues, proceeds from "an emotionally pre-Oedipal female-centered natural world to the heterosexual male world. . . . But the textual locus of this development . . . is a buried *sub*text that endures throughout the domestic and romantic plots of the foreground. In contemporary feminist fiction, the maternal plot is likely to be more insistently inscribed."[91] In contemporary women's fiction the foregrounded plot is equally likely to have to do with professional economic success as with romantic and domestic arrangements, these foregrounded plots having a double subtext—a romantic one and a maternal one.

In *Women of Academe: Outsiders in the Sacred Grove*, Aisenberg and Harrington explore the relationship of the marriage plot to women's place in the academy and suggest, although they do not use such language, that a maternal subplot both complicates and contests women's peculiar situation in our institutions as well as explains career choices that have resulted in their being "deflected," in some cases, that is, displaced from the tenure track.[92] In the picture that develops out of Aisenberg's and Harrington's interviews and interpretations we can detect traces of the Minoan civilization. The traces of pre-Oedipal attachment that appear in all of the stories lead to conclusions revealing fundamental institutional inhospitality to those women who do not choose unambivalently for the father. Authority is a principal problem for all of the women in the study, both in their teaching and in their scholarship. With respect to both, they appear unable to engage in the kind of distance that would yield total authorial control and at the same time permit them to make decisions based wholly on careerism. None of the stories can be read simply as pointing to a lack of role models or of female networks.

Jane's story recapitulates the female dilemma in making the transition from pre-Oedipal to Oedipal reality in a patriarchal world. The lost civilization must remain lost and the connection Jane longs for denied. Her relationship to Professor Cope must be mediated by the tools of scholarship and legitimated by them. The relationship must vanquish the missing but persistent third. Their relationship is mediated by the male voice, the voice of scholarly authority. Jane finds that she can neither speak in that voice nor silence it.

Jane's story is complicated by her having been raised by rejecting and self-centered parents. She compensates for her familial loss by her self-invented brilliance. She masters the language of the father; she moves easily in the public world. But she fears that she is a fraud, and she resents that her legitimacy inheres in her adopting another's story—Carryl Cope's story of the price of brilliance. And Jane is angry. Rather than choose silence or confrontation, though, she exaggerates what she thinks of as her fraud by undertaking to do explicitly that which she has always suspected herself of doing. In response to Lucy's accusation that Jane has chosen to throw Carryl to the wolves, Jane says: "What a sell for her! The infant prodigy turns out to be a fake!"[93] And Carryl at another time says, "Where did I go wrong? What happened? Am I crazy to think that for Jane Seaman to behave as a thief is a personal attack; that, consciously or not, it is an attack on me?" To which Lucy responds:

> Jane said it was like taking jumps on a horse with the bars set higher and higher. My guess is that at some point she went into panic. Possibly she realized without really knowing it that something was being left out; perhaps she wanted something of you quite desperately that you could not afford to give. It's not that she was right, only that she was stuffing herself with the wrong food and suffering from malnutrition if you like.[94]

On the surface, the story of Jane's plagiarism is a story of the relationship between institutions and individual responsibility, a story of the tension between authority and caring. It is complicated, though, by a mother-daughter subtext. The tensions in the foregrounded plot are fairly standard in novels about education. But rather than the novel's being about individual development—Jane does not mature in the ordinary sense—it is a novel about the adjustment of others in the institution to a criminal act by one of its members, about their complicity in that act. Appleton is a patriarchal institution, and the tragedies which its members live are the sacrifices demanded by patriarchy—the price of genius or excellence. Jane is caught in the story of the price of excellence, but it is not her story. The story of the price of excellence is the story that Lucy and her colleagues must rewrite if they are to teach young women and if they are to achieve their own voices in the institution.

Carryl Cope is a surrogate patriarch. She embodies the authority of institutions and disciplines, and it is she through whom that authority is passed on. She has never married, nor will she, having chosen to love another woman rather than men. Jane Seaman (semen) is as close as Carryl will come to having a child of her own; Professor Cope is Pygmalion, but her creation goes wrong, will never come to life and satisfy her desire. Carryl's friend says of her, "Carryl is like a man, of course. . . . I think Carryl saw in that girl, the image of herself when she was young."[95]

Jane's rebellion, like Dora's, is a struggle for the word. But her rebellion is also a peculiarly female one, one turned against herself, one that insures her expulsion from the institution against which she rebels. Jane's theft of another's words reveals her anomalous position within the institution, an institution which demands of women that they enact the father's stories, that they take those stories as their own.

Lucy learns in the course of the novel to attend to the subtext of women's lives and to foreground the subtext of her own. Only when she is able to do so is she able to commit herself to teaching. Lucy manages to survive what another character describes as the poison of "this atmosphere of self-mutilation,"[96] and is able in the end to assert her own need for both profession and belonging and to say, "If I stay, it will be for love."[97] And so does Carryl, but only through a special act of attention in which she comes to understand the sense in which, as she says, "Teaching women is a special kind of challenge. Most of the cards are stacked against one."[98]

I teach *The Small Room* in my philosophy of education course. Students in that course are required to write three 2–3 page papers pointing up an interesting or important question or problem in any of the books in the course. The only stipulation is that the papers be turned in in advance of the day that we begin class discussion of them. Most students in the course choose *The Small Room* as one of their three texts. The gender difference in responses is fascinating. Male students focus on the question of plagiarism and the appropriate institutional response. They want to talk about punishment and justice, about contracts and responsibility. Female students want to talk about the student-teacher relationship, about Lucy's resistance to the caring role and about the particular emotional neediness of Pippa, another and not so brilliant student at Appleton. Both of these thematics *are there in the text.* Which is the most important one? That question is one that we discuss in some detail. I argue that the answer to that question depends on what you understand, in Fish's language, to be the standard story. What is so bad about plagiarism? When we raise that question in class, we do so in order to reveal the subtexts of our two available standard stories. Neither of these questions are to be concluded. The point is to explore the institutional assumptions governing our reading and to locate our positions as readers. In this way we, men and women both, learn to speak together, to question, not in order to answer, but in order to understand.

If we would make our institutions more humane places for women (and consequently for men as well), we must learn to attend to the maternal subtexts in women's lives. We must fashion stories in which the word ceases to function only as a mark of loneliness and separation, pregnant with the possibility of betrayal. Excellence is too dear if its price is the pain of isolation and the fear that one's identity is a pose. If the word, our stories, are to grant us the power to forge relationships rather than to compensate for the loss of the originary maternal relationship, we must find new forms and a new language.

The female artist manque, having no medium of her own, makes of herself a work of art within the silent spaces allotted to her. She becomes her mother, and, as work of art, she makes of herself an object of aesthetic and erotic desire. For this reason women's art will always be personal, having a nearness to the self denied in the fathers' stories, but understood as the subtext and source of anxiety of those stories. The male artist creates in order to produce and control the Other; the female artist creates herself. Women's stories of the art of teaching, like Lucy Winters', must produce, as they acknowledge, this difference.

A Different Story

"Call me (not Ishmael) Mary Beton, Mary Seton, Mary Car-michael, or by any name you please—it is not a matter of any importance."[99] In order to talk about women and fiction, Virginia Woolf found herself obliged to invent a new literary form and to reexamine the literature we have. *A Room of One's Own* is an essay. But it is an essay with a fictional narrator—Mary Beton, Mary Seton, Mary Carmichael. Essays do not ordinarily have fictive narrators, nor do their authors take their names to be of little importance. But then the narrator of this essay, a narrator who at its opening has been refused admission to the library at Oxbridge on account of her gender, wonders whether it isn't perhaps worse to be locked in than to be locked out. This is also a narrator who remarks of all those women writers who used the names of men, "Anonymity runs in their blood. The desire to be veiled still possesses them. They are not even now as concerned about the health of their fame as men are, and, speaking generally, will pass a tombstone or a signpost without feeling an irresistible desire to cut their names on it, as Alf, Bert or Chas. must do in obedience to their instinct."[100]

The fictive narrator of *A Room of One's Own* is all women. She is the subject, the I, the writer of this essay, as she is its subject (object) which she announces as "W" or woman. Susan Gubar has argued that all women writers have been simultaneously the subject and the object of their art, denied the distance from the object safeguarded to their brothers, those creators of well-wrought urns. Virginia Woolf uses the denial of access to the library as a figure for her being denied access to the essay form, to the structures of language and knowledge of Professor Sherlock and his colleagues. To try to speak through the essay would be plagiarism. In speaking for Carryl Cope, in the idiom of excellence which threads through the discourse of Appleton, Jane Seaman committed plagiarism. Virginia Woolf creates a fictive narrator and uses time and space novelistically in this essay in order to get us to think about the form itself. Woolf's ambition is to feminize the essay, to make it congenial to women's voices, by adopting the conventions of that genre which has been most congenial to women's lives—the novel.

The fictive narrator of this novelistic essay hints that she might have written a proper essay but that as she was chasing a fugitive thought on the nature of art through her mind while walking rapidly across a grass plot,

> . . . instantly, a man's figure rose to intercept me. Nor did I at first understand that the gesticulations of a curious-looking object, in a cut-away coat and evening shirt were aimed at me. His face expressed horror and indignation. Instinct rather than reason came to my help; he was a beadle; I was a woman. This was turf; there was the path. Only the Fellows and Scholars are allowed here; the gravel is the place for me.[101]

The beadle intervenes. The forces of the male world that exclude women intervene. What in the male world has stopped the female essayist? It is the male's total appropriation of form and content both. But the small room of the essay with its confining attention to facts and to truth and to grand conclusions is itself a fiction, a fiction in which men have created women only in relation to men as they have in their poems and plays and novels. *A Room of One's Own* is, above all, a new form and one which contains a new sort of truth, one which creates a new sort of relationship between the author and her life and her work. We feminists run the risk now, of canonizing Virginia Woolf, of reifying her forms and truths. To do so would be to succumb once again to the seductions of patriarchy and to deny Woolf's own admonition against honors and distinctions.

The relationship between the author and her work, as it has always been between women writers and their work, is a personal one. Mary Beton, Mary Seton, Mary Carmichael rejects the old artistic molds and forms because these molds and forms distort our understanding of women, of men, and of art. Suppose, she says, all we knew of the male world we had learned from the female domestic novel. Suppose that all men knew of themselves they had learned from the ways that women have seen men in their relationship to women. And yet that is precisely how we women have come to know ourselves through the art in which we are represented, through the language in which we represent ourselves. It is precisely this art that we teach when we practice the art of teaching. In teaching women, we lead them into exile, giving them up to the forms and languages of the fathers. The forms and languages of the arts we employ frighten us with their contradictory appeals to integrity and their insistence on solitariness and division. Was there ever a creature more riddled with self-doubt?

Those who talk about the art of teaching often engage in, or urge the rest of us to engage in, an analysis of the art of teaching analogous to analyses of other art forms. Those forms and their analyses, however, leave out the experience of women teaching women and avoid our gendered modes of making art. To confront the classroom as a text or other object of art requires us to understand woman as object of art and to posit a woman reader of that art. Such a reader might ask, "What is so dreadful about plagiarism? What has been stolen or violated?"

Man is a creature of passion who must live out that passion in the world. What is the passion about and what is the source of the despair that reverberates through his insistence? That it is a cry of despair as well as an assertion, I have no doubt. I am certain that, knowing the history of my own relationship with that creature of passion, at the moment that I inscribed that cry into my notebook it was as a treasured confession from a lover, the artist who alone possesses the creative power to animate me. He was my teacher.

In Gubar's reading of the male creative myth, his desire is for the power to create the one who must love and totally comprehend him, a power of creation which the male artist usurps from woman. She who in her own corporealness is opaque must be made transparent. Her transparency is achieved by the artist's conception of her as empty. Gubar brings to us the words of male artists describing woman as a blank page, a page waiting to receive the writer's imprint. The male appropriation of the female body as the object of art results perforce in an aesthetic of distance. The object, however fashioned as a mirror of the artist's ideal, remains irredeemably, intractably Other. His passion and his despair are unassuaged. In response, Gubar tell us, women have taken themselves as texts, their bodies as objects out of which to create art. Necessarily, then, a woman's art is a personal one, one which collapses distance. Hers is an aesthetic of nearness. Rather than creating an idealized or despised Other, the female artist creates herself.[102] But still her language is the language of the fathers, and the stories that she tells observe their narrative conventions.

When we practice the art of teaching, we engage in the art of telling and embellishing stories we have read. We teach our students to read. We now suspect that reading and storytelling are gendered activities. Like our art, our education denies us access to female experience. That such is the case has been amply demonstrated in research on women and education. Our education either disvalues experiences and qualities which psychologists have taught us to associate with the female, ignores them, or reshapes them. It is an education which requires of us all that we look on the world from the distance safeguarded by the Law. It is an education which denies the personal, and one which denies the body—the body about which we women learn to become so acutely self-conscious. It is an education which denies the knowledge that we are limited in what we can know. The privileging of the invisible over the visible, of inference over intuition, is a consequence of the forever to be frustrated passion to claim with certainty the elusive object of desire—the knowledge of the-one-presumed-to-know.

According to Luce Irigaray, in the end the male project requires an unspoken denial of gendered difference. This denial of difference, she says, amounts to a denial of the legitimacy of woman's experience of herself, her only legitimate way of knowing her place in the world being through men's experience of her. The woman's project, as psychoanalyst, as teacher, as artist, says Irigaray, is to reclaim women's experience by producing difference in discourse, by multiplying voices. She urges us to have a fling with the philosophers by challenging all of their systems and ideas.[103] What is so awful about plagiarism?

In the spirit of Irigaray, it seems to me that we should reexamine what we take for granted about educational life. Why is plagiarism considered a more heinous act than nearly anything else a student might do? At Appleton plagiarism meant expulsion. Of course, it is true that universities are centers of intellectual work, that our work as teachers is to help students to achieve their full intellectual capacity and to teach them to think and write honestly. I am not condoning plagiarism. Rather, I am trying first to explore the possibility that a female student's plagiarism may have psychological and political dimensions not previously considered. Second, I mean to remind us that university preparation, at least according to the catalogues of liberal arts colleges and universities, is usually declared by professors and administrators to embody aims in addition to those having to do with the life of the mind. I should like us to ask ourselves why we do not punish other student transgressions of the aims and values of our institutions as drastically as we do plagiarism.

Disrespect of self and others, disregard for the future of the planet, failure to take social and political responsibility, moral apathy, spiritual enslavement to fashion or anything else—such things as these seem to me subversive of educational goals, for it seems to me that a sense of respect and regard ought to be a principal educational goal. In fact, if we look at any college catalogue description of the liberal arts project, we find enumerated such cares as I have listed. And yet the structure of our institutions, the laws, the regulations and the regularities, the form and content of our teaching place all of those cares beneath what we may take as a concern to protect private property. For knowledge has come to be a sort of property, just as women are, and plagiarism infringes on property rights. But more important than the status of knowledge as private property, I think, is our expectation that knowledge do more than it can. Suppose that Jane's plagiarism is a denial of property relations and an assertion of the limits of patriarchal knowledge. We academics tend to think, naively, that to know the good is to do it. We suppose that the truth will set us free. And knowledge, we hope, will heal the narcissistic wound, will assure us our integrity. It is for this reason that we confront plagiarism with such horror. But when our knowing is an act of splitting, then it becomes unclear what plagiarism is. At Appleton, the language and knowledge contained in the narratives of the values and commitments of the community for whom that language and knowledge served as the single mode of discourse is undermined finally by the exclusion of women from those narratives—by inattention to the maternal subtexts of the stories of what teachers and students are like. The cards are stacked against us because of what is foregrounded in our narratives and what is denied, split off, but which nonetheless complicates the foregrounded story.

Women's art denies that splitting, as ought women's teaching. The primary task of women teaching women (and men) is to enact a language and an art in which we all can converse as ourselves and in which the intellectual and emotional in each of us remain in conversation. We are reminded of Young-Bruehl's dream of a democratic mind.[104] The conversation among the elements of the democratic mind defies the patriarchal project of subordination and repression and moves us toward the liberatory ends of education. We may say that practicing the art of teaching is practicing the art of conversation, the subtleties and intricacies of which women are well-attuned to.

We do not plead for a rejection of the rational or the inferential. Nor do we mean to devalorize the experience of that creature of passion, our brother. Rather, we plead for a conception of art and education that opens the door to other rooms, and larger. In these larger rooms, the solitary singer might find a choir, the lonely teller of tales, that ancient mariner, an audience and a cast of characters on whose solidity and integrity he may depend. Such a conception would not deny difference, nor would it insist on unity. Such a conception would not deny the personal, would not deny the body. It would enable us to bring ourselves to our art and our education, both for ourselves and for others.

"If I stay, it will be for love," Lucy says. The story of the art of teaching, when it is practiced by women and when it is practiced in the teaching of women must begin by producing difference, by acknowledging what women know. Either we are locked out or we are plagiarists. The stories that we tell are not our own. The impulse to the art of women teaching and the art of teaching women begins in that recognition. The impulse is triggered by the recognition that our public standing, our excellence as scholars and teachers, exacts from us a different sort of pain, the pain of self-effacement. The possibilities of teaching as a woman depend on the possibilities of inscribing our practice within a larger textual system. I have tried to do that here with plagiarism by inscribing it within a system of violence and isolation and by elaborating the complexities of a single act, an act which proves to be, among other things, a gendered one.

7

Household Language and Feminist Pedagogy

> . . . women soon come into
> opposition to civilization. . . .
> Women represent the interests of
> the family and of sexual life. The
> work of civilization has become
> increasingly the business of men, it
> confronts them with ever more
> difficult tasks and compels them to
> carry out instinctual sublimations
> of which women are little capable.
> . . . Thus the woman finds herself
> forced into the background by the
> claims of civilization and she adopts
> a hostile tendency towards it.
> —Sigmund Freud,
> *Civilization and Its Discontents.*

From the time I began thinking systematically about curriculum and teaching, I have been convinced that discourse in the field is discourse about discourse. To talk about education is to talk about talk. But it is more than the "mere talk." The sort of talk I have in mind is properly called "conversation," and not idle conversation either. Theory and practice are two voices in a conversation. Teachers and students are others. The word "conversation" in its most primary sense has to do with acting and living among others. Conversation is not just chitchat over tea and cookies; to engage in conversation is to inflect oneself toward the Other. Conversation is made up of gesture and posture as well as of word. Conversation implies the several dimensions of community. A community is most obviously a linguistic commu-

133

nity, and a linguistic community is a speculum of a moral community. We learn to speak only as members of communities. Through education we enter a cultural conversation that is already taking place. We make representations in a world which is already represented for us. When we speak we claim our places in it, and we claim our connection to others. Debates in education are debates over legitimate representation and over who has or ought to have the power to represent. The one who speaks claims authority to speak.

Conversations may take place at nearer and greater distances — physical, psychological, intellectual, historical, and social. We converse with our loved ones, our colleagues, our students. We enter into conversations with the authors of books. A conversation may be an affirmation of intimacy, or it may be a business transaction only. The process of education takes place through conversation. In conversation one takes one's place. Or perhaps one is put in one's place. Conversation is not necessarily liberatory, although our inclinations are to think that it is. We have only to think of all of those representations which have held us all in thrall for centuries.

In conversation we make a world out of a common cultural stock of images. We make stories together. You and I are together, and one of us mentions our absent friend. We say he is unhappy. He sets his sights too low, we say, his ambition is too modest. It's his strange mix of competitiveness and insecurity, we say. He wants too badly to win, we say, and is too fragile to survive second-best. You and I are educated people. We see beneath the surfaces of things; together we make a story and interpret it. What do we actually *know* about him? Would he recognize himself in this story? We represent our absent friend in the images available to us from our common past. We read all the same books, after all. You and I discuss a colleague's most recent essay. He's very angry, we agree. That essay was absolutely written out of anger and fear. Would he recognize himself in our story, I wonder? Does it matter?

I have tried to locate a feminine position in the educational conversation. Too often the speakers in our conversation are aligned with the masculine interest even if they happen to female. Do we recognize ourselves in these stories? Does it matter? In the stories that dominate our cultural scene women have either been absent or objects of representation; we have been transformed into objects of male desire. To locate ourselves as women in those stories, in those representations, is to lose ourselves. And yet women have always told stories, even when they weren't allowed a formal education.

In doing feminist theory, we retell and analyze these stories in order to make for ourselves a heritage. Rather than letting our conversations with each other be mediated by the male standard story, we claim our own and speak directly to one another. Doing feminist theory is to act self-consciously as part of a community. Doing feminist theory we eschew any privatized notion of originality and claim as clearly as we can our antecedents and our contemporaries. We make ourselves known to ourselves by making ourselves known to each other. We assert connection. We claim difference. Feminist theory is inseparable from feminist pedagogy. To theorize is to teach and to teach from a feminist perspective is to theorize our connections and our differences.

I have always been fascinated by language. To make a world on a page or in the telling seemed always to me a magical act. My first encounters with anything have always provoked in me the impulse to tell all about it. Education too has also always been vitally important to me. Without my teachers, I know that my life would be immeasurably poorer. Perhaps it was my working-class background that made language and education matters of such grave importance to me. My parents' parents were immigrants, and I retain to this day the immigrant's faith in education. But when I went to school, I traveled a greater distance from my home than anyone knew. I felt myself moving between two languages in each of which my other life was secret. I learned to keep the distances secret. In the public codes of the school I entered the secrets of literature and art and music. In the private codes of home I kept the secrets of my family's difference from the middle-class kids and teachers I spent the day with. I loved my school and my library even though they took me from my home and even though I was always vaguely uneasy in those places. Even as a college student in my mid-twenties I struggled with the discomfort of those who feel out of place in the places they have taken. And things were no more comfortable at home. I had secrets, and these were the secrets of my own inferiority, my own pretence of being a native speaker anywhere. I was a liar, an impostor, a conversational dangler. This is the hidden injury of class that Richard Sennett and Jonathan Cobb described in the

1970s. It is also the hidden injury of sex. For an educated woman speaker/reader travels far from her own body, stands outside and scrutinizes it and keeps hidden inside her the secret of her femaleness. She learns to speak the impersonal language of scholarship. She learns to lie. She learns to tell the stories of her life as if her being a woman had nothing to do with her life. The secret of femaleness is the secret of her inferiority. And yet I still believe it better to speak than to be silent.

As a graduate student, I hoped to find a native tongue among the discourses of Marxism. There I thought I found my history named. I learned to call myself working class and to be proud of that history. Like many others, I tried to identify a role for the working-class intellectual. My working-class background is crucial to my work. But not because I am a working-class intellectual. That designation is disingenuous if not a downright contradiction in terms. My working class background is vital to my work precisely because I am no longer working class. The language I speak is that of the educated middle classes, and the story of my life is refracted through that language. But I am not middle class either in the same way as are my colleagues who were born into the language in which the cultural conversation takes place. Our places are different. It is not simply a matter of cultural capital. Whether one speaks as a native or an exile or refugee makes a difference. And not because the language is different, but because the speaker's relationship to the language is different.

The explorers of the hidden curriculum during the 1970's unveiled the secrets of the school—that the curriculum in content and form obeys the imperatives of capitalist production. They exposed the ways in which schools worked to reproduce the dominant culture both through what is present in the curriculum and through what is absent. Educational systems, we learned, are ideological arms of the capitalist state which perform the labor of turning out a properly socialized and stratified workforce. And indeed schooling has that effect. But . . .

The hidden curriculum of hidden curriculum research conceals in its disclosure of the political agenda of the curriculum, the personal agenda which is its other side. Just as the father infers his paternity through a series of resemblances and a system of rules for interpreting those resemblances so as to claim his child, so our curriculum knowledge and our knowledge about that curriculum is a representation of a phallocentric universe. The phallocentric system of differences and samenesses that permits us to distinguish self from Other, mothers from fathers, and deal children around to the proper parents, supports this enterprise. I do not mean to deny that class distinctions obey the patriarchal imperative. But even as we busy ourselves with sorting our objects in "this" and "not-this", we betray the persistence of that primal and unattainable desire for merging, for being given back ourselves immediately in the maternal gaze. That first knowledge of connection is repressed in service of the second knowledge of separation. With what consequences do we acquiesce in that repression? We betray ourselves at every turn. For the impulse to exploration of that dark continent of the hidden curriculum is a desire to deny the differences—intellectual, etc., presumed produced by the surface curriculum. What is repressed in the unconscious always returns. The image of the school as a sorting machine hints that difference is produced in experience as an artifact of the curriculum. Implicitly this denies difference, or at least denies the importance of difference in the structure of consciousness.

The structure of the curriculum itself, whether surface or hidden, is determined to deny connection. The dominant modes of reason—assimilation and analogy—pervade the curriculum and pervade hidden curriculum analyses. "Note three differences and three similarities between the French and American Revolutions." "The school is like a factory." "For learning to occur the child must possess a prior schema to which new knowledge can be assimilated." "How is a raven like a writing desk?" Even those who are aware that treating all children the same, because of the fact of produced difference, may be unequal or unfair, implicitly assume that different treatments are desirable in order to enable all children to achieve the same standards.[105] Whether the relationship between school and society is figured as mirror-like or mediational, the Rule of the One, of the logocentric rational, governs. Difference can be appreciated and celebrated only when connection is claimed. When I talk about connection, I do not mean to suggest the desirability of merging. The primitive desire to merge is expressed in the modes of assimilation and analogy which work to repress that desire. To be connected is not to be same as. To be different is not to be less powerful than, less worthy than, less present than. Difference need not be shameful, but it will continue to be so long as connection is repressed. The shame of difference and the shame of connection seem to exist side by side in women, particularly if sexual difference is combined with ethnic, racial, or class difference. Maxine Hong Kingston describes just such a double shame in *The Woman Warrior*.[106]

I do not mean to deny the emancipatory moment of hidden curriculum research or of the Marxist modes of analysis in which it is embedded. Still, to identify myself as a "working-class intellectual" or, for that matter, as a "feminist teacher" makes me uneasy. It seems that when I do so, I sentimentalize my history. It seems that when I do so I claim for myself an ideological purity which entitles me to dominate all discussion, to silence dissent. It seems to me that we must resist our tendencies to make of theory a totalizing story of the universe. Feminist work may be patriarchal too.

Just as the analytic philosopher must have a world lined up in ordered oppositions, so does the Marxist scholar. So too do many versions of feminism. Many feminist theorists have argued that sex oppression is the fundamental and prior one and the model for all oppressions. Marxists argue that class is the primary oppression. Marxist feminists and feminist Marxists sometimes have a hard time with each other. As if it mattered which came first. As if there were only two kinds of things in the world.

I think of all the films I've seen (for some reason I think of them all as starring either Steve McQueen or Paul Newman) during the course of which some character has announced that there are only two kinds of people in the world: the winners and losers, the givers and the takers, the cons and the fallguys, etc. We are grateful to Sergio Leone who gave us not only the good and the bad, but the ugly right along with them. Well, there are two kinds of people in the world—those who speak and those who are silent.

"Emancipatory" rhetoric, as we know, can conceal just as much as it reveals. It can be used to enslave and repress. My knowledge and not yours. My oppression and not yours. I think of my own treatment of Kevin in the events leading up to "Practical Fictions." I wonder how many students I have silenced in the name of freedom, justice, and equality. I wonder how many colleagues I have silenced. The emancipatory rhetoric of certain critical theoretical positions colludes with patriarchy. It is difficult living in our cultural institutions to avoid that. Living in the

institution particularly charged with the production and reproduction of culture—the university—is particularly difficult. And when
they start letting us speak at conferences, the seductions of
patriarchal reward systems may seem irresistible. It seems that
participating in those institutions entails that we give ourselves up
to the logic of master and slave as it is instantiated in all of our
oppositions. I am a female professor. I make my way up through
the academic ranks. I stand for tenure. I sit on committees. I make
decisions about others, colleagues as well as students. I act to
certify male knowledge even as I am constructed as an object of
that knowledge, even as I become a figurative substitute for my
literal self. I owe my position to my having made my way through
patriarchal structures. My position is defined by patriarchal
arrangements. Was there ever a life more riddled with self-doubt
than that of the female professor?

The metaphor of voice in education is a persistent one. The
educational project, we are inclined to say, has as its aim authentic
and empowered speaking. Those concerned with achieving
humane ends in this world talk often about the deprivation of
voice as the ultimate evil. Those who are prevented from
speaking, those who are excluded from language, those whom
Freire refers to as members of the "culture of silence," are
deprived of the power to act on the world. They are deprived of
authority. They are deprived of the power to inscribe their lives in
the world. They are robbed of their histories and their bodies.

The history of education in democratic societies has been a
history of inclusion. Educational reform in this country has often
meant the extension of certain educational goods to those who
had been previously excluded. The common school movement,
the secondary school movement, land grant colleges, state
universities and community colleges have all in one sense
"democratized" education, as have various curriculum reforms. In
the process of inclusion, those of us who have been able to do so
have accommodated ourselves to the institutions which admitted
us and have been assimilated as we have adopted assimilation and
analogy as our dominant mode of reason. But just as assimilation
in the realm of reason, in devalorizing difference, expresses the
more primitive desire to merge in repressing the knowledge of
connection, so institutional assimilation excludes both difference
and connection. When I am included in patriarchal institutions,

my gendered difference is denied, excluded from the realm of relevance.

We know that traditionally women have been excluded from public authority—that is from access to public language used for public purposes. We know with what horror the brothers and fathers and husbands of nineteenth-century feminists and abolitionists witnessed their public speech-making even while supporting the causes. We know, with some exceptions, of course, that when women have not been excluded from authorship, their work has been devalorized. Those whom Virginia Woolf referred to as "educated men's daughters" were totally without value in the public world except as ornament to their fathers' and husbands' success. But we have now been assimilated. "[We] can bring home the bacon and fry it up, too, and never let him forget he's a man."[107] We can now give commands, and we can suffer the stresses of success.

Woolf thought that when women gained access to public institutions, when we were no longer locked out and forbidden entrance to the library at Oxbridge, when we gained 500 pounds and rooms of our own, we would find our voices. At the same time, she knew that admission to the library may be a mixed blessing. She knew that we should likely have to leave our own experience as sisters and daughters and mothers at the library door. She knew that there was always the danger that our altos and sopranos would vanish in the depths of our fathers' basso profundos and be overwhelmed by our brothers' mellifluous tenors. She knew that we might find ourselves trapped in an indeterminate universe in which we ourselves are all too determinate.

We now have access to education. We participate in the public ceremonies and parades that Virginia could only watch from her window. We wear the robes of office. The power to give commands belongs to some of us. Certainly our history has ill-prepared us for this power. "Take off your muddy boots," is scarcely equivalent to, "Thou shalt not covet thy neighbor's wife," or "All men are created equal." Still, we do acquire the habit of public command. Ought we to want what we have?

The education to which we have access and the power that we exercise maintain the structures of dominance and submission which sustain patriarchal rule. Fifty years ago Virginia Woolf asked us to consider whether this is the education we want and whether it is the one we ought to want:

> Now we are here to consider facts; now we must fix our eyes upon the procession—the procession of the sons of educated men. There they go, our brothers who have been educated at public schools and universities, mounting those steps, passing in and out of those doors, ascending those pulpits, preaching, teaching, administering justice, practicing medicine, transacting business, making money. It is a solemn sight, this procession, a sight that has often caused us, you may remember, looking at it sidelong from an upper window, to ask ourselves certain questions. But now, for the past twenty years or so, it is no longer a sight merely, a photograph, or fresco scrawled upon the walls of time, at which we can look with merely an aesthetic appreciation. For there, trapesing [sic] along at the tail end of the procession, we go ourselves. We who now agitate these humble pens may in another century or two speak from a pulpit. . . . Who can say whether, as time goes on, we may not dress in military uniform.[108]

Who are these educated men, these busy leavers of home for the real world places from which power issues and commands are made? What is it to be an educated man? This is a question familiar enough to us all. The answers too are familiar to us all. We know about cognitive capacity, about disposition to knowledge, about breadth of knowledge, about disciplines and -ologies and -osophies. We know that answering this question is important. We know (we have been taught by the philosopher) that if we would educate we must first know what it is to be educated. Thought and definition, we know, are always foundational to action. Woolf teaches us to ask what is required of the educated daughter of educated men. She also teaches us to ask what is possible.

Fifty years ago, Virginia Woolf urged us to think about whether we wanted to join that procession and on what terms. She counseled us to think where it might lead us. She imagined a future in which educated men's daughters would receive the education denied herself and her sisters. Ten years earlier, imagining for us rooms of our own and dinners with fine wine, she led us on a journey from Oxbridge to Fernham to the British Museum where she introduced us to the specular ladies imagined by the educated men. She introduced us too to the women writers

who had managed to speak and acquainted us with the cost of
their speaking. Later she recalled for us her own struggle to write.
It demanded of her a labor similar to that demanded of the woman
teacher, I think. She must kill the "angel in the house:"

> She [the angel] was intensely sympathetic. She was immensely
> charming. She was utterly unselfish. She excelled in the difficult
> arts of family life. She sacrificed herself daily. If there was a
> chicken, she took the leg; if there was a draught she sat in it—in
> short she was so constituted that she never had a mind or a wish
> of her own, but preferred to sympathize always with the minds
> and wishes of others. . . . And when I came to write I encountered
> her with the very first words. The shadow of her wings fell on my
> page; I heard the rustling of her skirts in the room. Directly, that is
> to say, I took my pen in my hand to review that novel by a famous
> man, she slipped behind me and whispered. "My dear, you are a
> young woman. You are writing about a book that has been written
> by a man. Be sympathetic; be tender; flatter; deceive; use all the
> arts and wiles of your sex." . . . Had I not killed her she would
> have killed me. . . . [T]he struggle was severe; it took much time
> that had better have been spent upon learning Greek grammar; or
> in roaming the world in search of adventures. . . . Killing the Angel
> in the House was part of the occupation of a woman writer.[109]

But what do we do with the corpse, Virginia? The unwashed
and unburied corpse of the angel haunts us all. If women do think
back through their mothers, what happens when they kill their
angel? She is correct in understanding that saying "I" requires us
to turn our backs on the imaginary mother-child dyad. We avert
our eyes from the maternal gaze where identity is first found and
align ourselves with the father's symbolic order. Are these our
only choices? Must we either stay at home or join the procession
of educated men? Woolf's writing itself shows us another way.
Her writing kicks over the institutional traces of difference and
sameness. It exposes the narcissistic wound, and refuses to be
assimilated to the rule of the one.

Language and the disciplines constituted by language emerge
from an absence first perceived as sexual difference. As Lacan
observed, though, entry of the third term—the phallus—into the
imaginary dyad has different effects for males and females.
Although the perception of sexual difference and the speaking
subject are both constituted in this moment of violence, the

violence experienced is different for sons and daughters. The son's desire for the mother is transformed into a quest for symbolic substitutes for the maternal body—for objects like the mother. The female body in its difference becomes one of these symbolic substitutions. The daughter's likeness to the maternal body permits her to remain connected to the literal maternal body, while at the same time, her entry into the symbolic transforms her into a substitute for her literal self.

In the symbolic order, the figurative, the inferential, the unseen figured in the mind's eye is the source of privilege, as Freud notes in *Moses and Monotheism*. Hence the superiority, both moral and rational, of one god—invisible and indivisible. In this order, the female body, that first object of the senses, remains rooted in the literal. The woman may be bearer of the word, but she cannot become the word. This relationship may have painful repercussions for the female speaker.

Woolf herself was, until the end of her life, ambivalent about the maternal heritage. Having dispatched her Angel, does the woman writer speak the male "I"? Sometimes Woolf seems to say "No." She reminds us of the incandescent mind of Jane Austen or savors the knowledge that Chloe liked Olivia, and that, moreover, they shared a laboratory.[111] We may after all learn Greek without violence, she seems to say. And yet that image of the lustrous procession, the generations of professors marching off to war in their academic regalia haunts and makes us pause. And we watch Minta Doyle lose her grandmother's brooch, recall her leaving her copy of *Middlemarch* on the train, and become engaged to be married, repudiating at once Mrs. Ramsey and George Eliot.[110] This is the tension that holds at the center of all of Woolf's work, and it is like the tension of the female professor, who, having joined the procession, still thinks back through her mothers, who recalls with yearning that journey through the British museum as we tried to imagine with Virginia Woolf an alternative literature and a sentence of our own. That journey announced to us the knowledge of our connection to other women, and the importance of our differences. Woolf felt as if she had made a major discovery when she discovered that Chloe and Olivia were friends. She has always pointed a way for us. In finding new forms, in redefining the novel and the essay, in taking us for walks and on bus rides and boat rides, she has literalized those figures which have excluded women and denied otherness.

"J'appelle un chat un chat."[112] Freud has just interrupted his account of Dora's nervous cough. He has just traced the origin of the mysterious cough to Dora's having witnessed a scene of fellatio between her father and Frau K. All of a sudden, Freud accuses the reader of horror and astonishment. I, the reader, am no doubt astonished he says, that a middle-aged man would speak to a young girl of such matters. I, the reader, am horrified, he says, that a young girl would possess any such knowledge as that in Dora's possession. Freud hastens to assure me that horror and astonishment both are misplaced. Gynecologists talk about such things with their patients all the time, he says. He is a scientist. He is dry and direct regarding such matters. He simply calls things by their proper names. "I call bodily organs and processes by their technical names, and I tell these to the patient if they—the names, I mean—happen to be unknown to her. J'appelle un chat un chat." Besides, as he tells us, the proper treatment of hysteria demands a discussion of sexual topics; "pour faire une omelette, il faut casser des oeufs."

Jane Gallop cleverly interprets this figurative turn, making an apparently innocent turn of phrase the key to understanding *Freud's* Dora.[113] Gallop argues, as have others, that Freud has a real problem with Dora. His problem is Dora's knowledge. Freud claims for himself merely the role of translator, Dora being the author of the nervous cough. Freud, as translator, tells us directly, simply, scientifically, what Dora's cough means. Having assured us that that is all he has done, he immediately turns to figurative, allusive, and downright suggestive language. Moreover, he does so in language not his own. (We should note that the English translator retains the French expression despite the availability of an English equivalent, "I call a spade a spade.") And in this foreign language, 'chat' or 'chatte' may be used as vulgar slang for the female genitalia. Freud, Gallop says, has called "a pussy a pussy." His real translation is from the literal to the figurative.

Meanwhile, Rousseau talked back to Plato. Our cultural heritage is figured large in their conversation. Reenacting the primal drama, the son refused to submit to the order of the fathers and determined to disrupt custom, convention, and convenience. His weapons against the state and order were nature and freedom. The repressed always returns. We are compelled to repetition—in our arts, in our sciences, in our law. The education we all have lived, the processions we have straggled in, the battles and the struggles, repeat over and over again the moment of violence when the phallus disrupts the imaginary dyad, exiling the mother to the register of silence, there to become an object but never a subject of representation.

Although, to be sure, Rousseau may be read as mounting a revolutionary challenge to Plato's conservative theory of education, he may also be read as relandscaping the patriarchal estate. The logocentric language of patriarchy is defined principally by its binary structure. In any set of paired oppositions one term is superior. Presence is superior to absence, inference is superior to sensory knowledge, reason to experience or emotion, objectivity to subjectivity, the one to the many. One god, one totalizing theory, one sexual organ. A world inscribed within such a logic is a world in which all speech occurs within relations of dominance and submission.

In the confrontation between the particular father and son, in this case Plato and Rousseau, similarity may prove more instructive than difference. Both the General Will and the Ideas are abstractions, mythologies obedient to a unifying logic. As Jane Roland Martin points out, both employ a production model of education.[114] Both divest women of power, although in different ways. Plato does it by making sex irrelevant, Rousseau by sentimentalizing femininity just as he does nature.

Derrida notes that both are engaged in a compensatory enterprise made necessary by the fact of speech.[115] He notes that both found writing inferior to speech because the absence of the writer multiplied the distance between signifier and signified. This distance hugely increases the possibility of misunderstanding. The myth of speech embedded in this judgment is one wherein the presence of the speaker serves somehow to guarantee on the part of the listener a perfect apprehension of the speaker's meaning. This myth is another expression of the romantic yearning behind "when-we-two-shall-be-as-one," when you give me back the self my mother took from me when she turned away.

Rousseau referred to writing in the same way that he referred to both education and masturbation—as a supplement. All are perverse additions—writing to speech, education to nature, and masturbation to "normal" sexual activity. Derrida argues that the logic of the supplement entails as a matter of logic an original lack.[116] Nature must be supplemented, completed by education if human nature is to emerge as it truly is. Derrida argues that speech, also, is a supplement. It is constituted out of a historical absence. Speech is a symbolic substitute for the exiled and absent mother and is the emblem of opposition and alienation. All of our distinctions—self-other, world-self, logos-eros—Derrida says, are divided against an apparent unity in speech. Unity is only apparent, though, and speech achieves this illusion because it bears a trace of the imaginary mother-child dyad. In speech one seems present to oneself. One cannot misunderstand oneself. There is no possibility of mistake here.

Most important in considering the family resemblances between Plato and Rousseau is, as Martin points out, the difference in their treatment of women's education.[117] This difference too is an apparent one. There is finally no difference in their feeling about women. While Rousseau argues that sex makes an enormous difference and has everything to do with determining right education, Plato is completely willing for women to receive a guardian's education should they participate in guardian nature. In this Plato has more in common with us than does Rousseau. But we ourselves in regarding as invidious distinctions of sex, betray as does Plato, fear of difference expressed in a logic of assimilation. Logocentrism is a logic of the same.

In the hierarchical opposition male-female, Plato and Rousseau both, as did Freud, treat the female as supplementary to or parasitic on the male. For Freud the male genitalia become the point of reference. The little boy sees what the little girls lacks, and the Oedipal moment is born in both children. The presence of the phallus is the norm, its absence an affliction. Until this moment, "the little girl is a little man." The phallus is the mark of privilege and that to which all must be assimilated. A woman who becomes a guardian transcends her affliction, her feminine nature, and speaks in the voice of patriarchal authority. Rousseau's female is irremediably castrated. There are no appliances to ease her affliction.

Whether guardian or wife, whether marcher in the procession or spectator, whether combatant or mourner of the dead, woman is displaced from the symbolic contract. Her displacement is its guarantee. Her literalness is its foundation. Her exile is its price. Only by relinquishing her femininity can a woman be signatory to the symbolic contract.

The various positions riding the current wave of educational reform can be read as embedded in the same logic. In that discourse all must be assimilated to the unitary phallic signifier or exiled to the maternal outland. Excellence is the master signifier in these discourses. Foundations are its guarantee. Core courses and cultural literacy, great books and economic competitiveness are the foundation and standard against which all knowledge and all learning are to be measured and judged. The speakers disdain concern for nurture and caring. Discipline and standardization take their place in order to insure greater *rigor* in our educational practices. And excellence is understood to be a unitary and objectively identifiable characteristic of objects, performances, and persons independent of context, purpose, or perception. All discourse is hierarchically structured. Difference is recognized only for purposes of value judgments. With these as conventions of the governing narratives in educational discourse, the outcomes are predictable. We will learn a great deal about institutional characteristics, about the demography of school populations and the teaching profession. The teaching profession itself will be standardized in the name of professionalism, and it will be organized along clear lines of command and subordination.

For all of the writers who have argued that the same educational treatment for all may be inherently unfair, the dominant discourse of the present moment insists all the more strenuously on common treatments. For all the writers and philosophers who have argued attention to dailiness, to personal understanding, to the large and small acts of signification, to the large and small acts of courage and cowardice which form the lives of children and teachers, for all that we have learned from these intentions, the dominant discourse tidies up the mess of human response and human diversity. But difference denied is difference enslaved. Difference repressed is bound to return. This is the hope of feminist theory and feminist pedagogy. We can produce the difference denied; we can resist both assimilation and the temptation to be *like* those in control, and by asserting our connection to our students, our colleagues, to the everyday, maintain connection and acknowledge difference.

The feminist project resembles the psychoanalytic in its confidence in the emancipatory potential of language. This might seem a foolish faith given all of the obstacles in our way. If language is an expression of repressed desire for the female body, a translation of that desire in service of the interest in dominating and controlling that body, we appear to be trying to say what, *in principle,* cannot be said. But that is because we have overlooked the fact that the household contains brothers and sisters as well as mothers and fathers.

In her search for emancipatory speech, Jean Elshtain takes us back to Plato.[118] She reminds us that women in ancient Greece had no *place* to speak, that is, they had no *public* forum for their thoughts. Their language, the private speech of the household, Plato said, was without meaning. It is the language of mere opinion, of appearances only. Meaning that leads to truth is the province of the language of the philosophical dialogue occurring in the marketplace and symposia, away from women.

Elshtain's interest is in developing in political theory a feminist discourse that rejects domination. Her project is one of uniting women. She seems to be arguing that the political theorists who have provided us with our models for theory, feminist theorists as well as those with other political affiliations, speak a language distorted by peculiarly male interests. She notes the prevalence of the discourse of self-interest in liberal political theory and its logically entailed divisiveness. She also notes the way in which the public language of such theory "flattens discourse" and reduces each of us to our roles. Theory works in just this way, I think, because of its rejection of private experience. Elshtain's faith in the emancipatory potential of speech is a faith in the possibility of a conversation between public and private, out of which new meanings might be produced. Elshtain believes that truth telling is possible, and that truth defies domination. She says truth is:

> speech that simultaneously taps and touches our inner and outer worlds within a community of others with whom we share deeply felt, largely inarticulate, daily renewed intersubjective reality.
>
> For women to affirm the protection of fragile and vulnerable human existence as the basis of a mode of political discourse and to create the terms for its flourishing as a worthy political activity, for women to stand firm against cries of "emotional" or "sentimental," even as they refuse to lapse into a sentimental rendering of values and language that flow from "mothering," would signal a force of great reconstructive potential.

In pedagogy as in politics, true speaking is our aim. Yesterday's *New York Times* crossword puzzle contained an interesting clue: "factual; faithful." This was the definition of "true." It seemed to me as I was solving the puzzle that that pairing summed up everything we mean to say about an emancipatory language. To speak truly is to speak faithfully as well as factually. Facts exist in the public sphere, faith in the private. In the word "true" the two meet. The truth is a matter of trust. The irony is, of course, that the truth, constructed as one truth, in one domain as foundational, is a substitute for that trust.

A feminist pedagogy is one in which the two meanings of "true" meet. A feminist pedagogy is faithful to the truth of home, faithful to the origins of truth in issues of dependence and independence (logocentric discourse often opposes "freedom" or "separation," sometimes interchangeably to dependence), and a feminist pedagogy is faithful to the truth of the agora and faithful to the facts. The discourse of pedagogy should shift from place to place and from position to position, taking up multiple relationships with multiple persons. The discourse of educational theory should make those same shifts, each position rediscovering itself and others over and over again. Our discourse should unfold conversation between household language and the language of the symposium, between the literal and the figurative. Each language provides a critical completion of the other. We must return our figures to the literal origins, fasten our words again to things if we are not to be forever lost in the wilderness of our figures. We must find the figures to express literal experience in our common search for liberation if we are not to remain exiled in the wilderness of our silence.

Virginia Woolf, in her search for a woman's sentence, reconstructed the project of fiction, found new forms for it, and endowed it with new concerns. She was able to inspirit her language with a literal otherness, to make a virtue of difference and multiplicity, to assert connections and to contest the totalizing tendencies of patriarchal discourse which repress the primitive desire to merge.

The discourse of education and of educational inquiry, to deliver on its emancipatory promise, must make present the concrete, the literal relationships of ourselves to language and to learning. The discourse must attend to the desire out of which language and learning emerge. An emancipatory educational discourse will learn to listen to itself and to others. We have let the word which was to bind us to ourselves take our places. A feminist pedagogy must reclaim the binding. Let that be our reason for coming into opposition to civilization, to bind but not subdue it. In the spaces between the literal and the figurative, we may hear the whispers of a household language which was our first reason for coming together. We found our culture first at home. It was there that we entered the conversation. In the meantime we may all dream of a truly common language:

> Vision begins to happen in such a life
> as if a woman quietly walked away
> from the argument and jargon in a room
> and sitting down in the kitchen, began turning in her lap
> bits of yarn, calico and velvet scraps,
> laying them out absently on the scrubbed boards
> in the lamplight, with small rainbow-colored shells
> sent in from cotton-wool from somewhere far away,
> and skeins of milkweed from the nearest meadow—
> original domestic silk, the finest findings—
> and the darkblue petal of the petunia,
> and the dry darkbrown lace of seaweed;
> not forgotten either, the shed silver
> whisker of the cat,
> the spiral of paper-wasp-nest curling
> beside the finch's yellow feather.
> Such a composition has nothing to do with eternity,
> the striving for greatness, brilliance—
> . . . .
> pulling the tenets of a life together
> with no mere will to mastery,
> . . . .

With no mere will to mastery, we learn to speak together. With no mere will to mastery, we may achieve the creative power of our own voices.

Postscript

In 1984 I spent six months in Budapest. I went to Budapest to be with my husband, who had been granted a Fulbright to support his work in translating Hungarian poetry. Neither of us knew any Hungarian at that time. Although he had been translating Hungarian poets for seven years, my husband had always worked from "roughs," that is from prose renditions of a poem prepared by a native "informant" who is also fluent in English. Prior to our departure for Hungary, he attended a "briefing session" in Washington D.C. The materials prepared about negotiating in the unfamiliar culture for visiting scholars suggested something like the following: "Encourage your family to learn some Hungarian. It's fun! And it will please the Hungarians." Neither of us was at all prepared for the shock of immersion. Having been very busy with our teaching and other obligations in addition to getting ready to spend half a year away from home, we had decided to defer, until our arrival there, the fun of learning some Hungarian. Other people's pleasure and our own, we thought, could wait until duty was satisfied.

We arrived in Budapest on New Year's day after an entire day and night of traveling. Fortunately, we were met at the airport by someone sent from the Ministry of Culture. Fortunately also that person was to spend three days helping us to settle into the flat we would call home for the next six months. No one spoke any English. Or even French, which we could have managed. And

151

only those above a certain age spoke German, which my husband can manage. This was true of all of those with whom we had dealings over the daily business of life. Even at the ministry I was directed to in order to prepare the papers that would permit me to reenter Hungary after attending a conference in the States, no one spoke English or anything else. I remember walking from room to room in a dark and heavy stone building, knocking at doors, being directed elsewhere. I could not figure out where I was being sent. I felt like Joseph K. I immediately regretted not having permitted myself the fun of learning some Hungarian the previous fall.

My mother tells a story about when I was two years old. I was small for my age and toothless and hairless. But I talked like mad, and I wanted to read. This combination of factors, my mother says, made me an object of wonder every time we rode the bus. I did not let my inability to read stop me from reading. I used to memorize advertisements on the buses and "read" them from one end of the bus to the other. I have never stopped reading signs. On my first taxi ride from the airport to our flat in Budapest I "read" every sign. And was terrified by the secrets of the signs denied to me, an illiterate. The first words I learned to recognize were the words meaning "Forbidden" and "Warning." It was terrifying to be unable to decipher what I was being forbidden or warned against.

Each day my husband went to an office where he worked with his informant. I took on the household duties of shopping and dealing with the laundry, etc. During the first weeks we had some comic meals put together out of my attempts to decode shop labels. Once I bought some sort of unidentifiable object which ended up in a sack for the dog next door. We had our dinner out that night and hoped that the smell in our flat would have dissipated by the time we returned home.

When I was not reading or writing at home, I spent my days walking the streets, riding the trams and buses, crossing and recrossing the bridges over the Danube, trying to learn the city. Sitting on the tram, I would hear snatches of conversation, not a syllable of which was accessible to me. Even native speakers have been known to say that Hungarian is an impossible language. It is certainly totally unlike any other, its nearest relative being Finnish, and it bears the same relationship to that that English does to Polish. During the first weeks, I was unable even to distinguish word and sentence divisions. I was silent—totally silent for the greatest portion of each day, and totally uncomprehending.

I began to reflect on stupidity. Suddenly I knew what it was to be stupid. It sometimes seemed to me that I had always been stupid. I felt the frustration and became accustomed to holding myself rigid against the humiliation. A great deal of the time I felt invisible in my stupidity. I existed for no one in that whole city. If by chance someone on the street or in the market offered a chance remark, I was dumb. I was erased from the pages of daily communication in my dumbness. As the stranger turned away, I felt myself begin to fade. When I began to acquire the language, I was never in public without fearing impatience and misunderstanding. To be unable to speak, to read, to understand, to live without the pleasures of conversation, intimate ones with friends, casual ones with the woman behind you in the supermarket line, is to be unable to name and define your own existence. I have since learned some Hungarian. And I suppose it's fun. I feel at home when I go there now, and I have friends. I even know the small guilty pleasure of eavesdropping on a train or in a cafe. Then it was much more a matter of survival.

During the time I was in Budapest, I wrote letters home—long ones. I wrote to my friends, my colleagues, my family—even to my thirteen-year-old niece who sent me cat and dog stickers in return. The mail was delivered twice daily, and I checked my box at least twice that often. "Letters home" carries a particular resonance for me now. Letters home were my connection to the world in which I did exist. There I was a sister, a daughter, a friend, an aunt. I was a university teacher who sometimes spoke at conferences and was sometimes believed. I was real and so was the language through which I expressed that reality. Letters home were also my way of defining the Hungarians. I could explain them, tell stories. In my letters home, I was an authority on the oddities of Hungarian life. Able to talk about Hungarian life in my own language, I existed. Would the Hungarians have recognized themselves in those stories, I wonder?

Through education we come to participate in making our culture's stories. We read the stories of our history. We learn to express ourselves in the common stock of cultural images. Or some of us do. Some of us just have stories told about us. In either case we take our places in those stories. But do we recognize ourselves in those stories? Who is telling them? Are we visible?

Are we stupid? Whose story is this anyway? The stupid are those deprived of stories, those who are objects and never subjects, those who are gossiped about in their absence and never gossip back.

It's all Greek to me. People attempting to describe feelings of stupidity, isolation, and powerlessness often resort to the figure of the foreign language or to images of objects severed from their meanings. Letters miscarrying and falling into the wrong hands have occasioned many catastrophes in literature as in life. Lies, innuendoes, misunderstandings and double-meanings are the hounds of tragedy. Stories of exile and loneliness, of the limits and inadequacies of language, tales of forgotten tongues in which the truth can be spoken, a truth in which one's self can be spoken and made visible, are part of our mythology. But men and women have told these stories differently for they occupy different places within them.

Civilization is desire sublimated. The child, to enter civilization, to participate in the cultural conversation, must move from the register of desire to the register of the symbol, from the presence of the mother to her absence. The symbol is resonant with homesickness. To speak, to acquiesce in the mother's absence, is to align oneself with the possessor of the phallus. Even for the girl who is condemned to resemble her mother. The woman's homesickness is a homesickness for herself, for the self that embodies the lost mother.

The conversations which take place in the chapters of this book are attempts to produce rather than deny difference. Producing difference, insisting on it, I hope to speak the unspeakable. The unspeakable is the fragility of the "I" in the absence of connection and implication. In these chapters I describe the felt stupidity of the exile who longs for the conversations she is convinced are taking place in cosy rooms behind doors closed to her. They are all about community and the finding and forming of community, about a person's membership in community. They are about knowledge and responsibility, about my knowledge and yours. They are about muteness and invisibility. They are about women who read, write, speak, and teach. But this book is not only about women. Since it is about women who teach, it is about women who hold conversation across generations with their fathers and brothers. It is about women who draw others, boys and girls, men and women, into that conversation. It is about what happens when a woman chooses to take her place in the cultural conversation with her fathers and brothers, attempting to speak from a feminine position.

This conversation is a conversation among exiles. We are all, men and women alike, exiles from the maternal body and homesick for the fullness of the mother's gaze. For in that gaze we are given to ourselves surely and wholly—visible. The brothers and fathers whom I meet in these pages, Plato and Nietzsche, Descartes, Rousseau and Wittgenstein and the others, the students and the colleagues, I meet as fellow exiles. We can acknowledge that connection among us, a connection first known in the connection to the mother. Our acknowledged connections to each other can defend against the primitive desire to merge. When Rousseau argues that writing is a "supplement" to speech, he reveals at one and the same time his longing for the immediate bodily knowledge of the maternal presence and his sense that that presence is itself incomplete—requires a supplement. His writing is a supplement to his own existence. I am trying in these pages to theorize the vulnerability of the practitioner, the one whom Wittgenstein would call the master of a language game. Vulnerability recognized and named, I think, pleads for alternative practice. At one level I have tried to model alternative practice. A phallocentric practice, a phallocentric pedagogy, demands an end; it demands closure. It demands exclusion and stupidity. It demands a world in which brothers compete over fathers' dead bodies and mothers demurely retreat to mourn the dead.

My homesick letters home from Budapest were written against my silence and against my invisibility. Funny sometimes, thoughtful often, always replete with absence and distance, these letters were conversations with the only people with whom I could speak. They were my conversation with absence. I have been fascinated since with the figure of the exile and images of homesickness. But the voiced exile is different from the silent one. In silence the body disappears. I have come to read this book as a conversation with homesick philosophies.

But as exiles, we can form our own communities. We can speak together a common language and make a home for ourselves in this world. Families are made up of sisters and brothers as well as of mothers and fathers. Perhaps Freud was too neglectful of the siblings. The talk among siblings surely contains greater possibilities for equality and authority, for freedom and community than that between parents and children. In patriarchal models of pedagogy, the father steps in. The father alone guarantees the child's individuality. In feminist models the siblings are there to remind us both of the original connection which we all share and of our individuality. The power of the Freudian myth blinds us to that. In the first story I told in "Teaching the Text" it is now apparent to me that my *sister* was there, prominently, and I was as afraid of losing her as I was of losing my mother and my home. The pages of this book are filled with the conversation of siblings and nieces and students and friends and colleagues. I discovered that only through listening to those past conversations. A teacher is a student. We speak together. We are connected and we are different. In that knowledge pedagogical discourse opens the world to the moral imagination and to humane practice.

Notes

1. Elaine Showalter, "Feminist Criticism in the Wilderness," in *Feminist Criticism: Essays on Women, Literature and Theory*, Elaine Showalter, editor (New York: Pantheon Books, 1985).

2. Jonathan Culler, *On Deconstruction* (Ithaca: Cornell University Press, 1982).

3. Virginia Woolf, *A Room of One's Own* (New York: Harcourt Brace Jovanovich, 1957).

4. The significance of the physical similarity of daughter to mother is what distinguishes both American object relations theory as developed by D. W. Winnicott and extended by Nancy Chodorow and Lacanian theory from orthodox psychoanalytic theory. This is particularly interesting in view of the fact much of Lacan's work is an assault on object relations theory.

5. Margaret Homans, *Bearing the Word: Language and Female Experience in Nineteenth-Century Women's Writing* (Chicago: The University of Chicago Press, 1986).

6. Madeleine R. Grumet, "On Daffodils That Come Before The Swallow Dares," Paper Presented at the Conference on Qualitative Inquiry, Stanford University, June 24–26, 1988.

7. *The Oxford English Dictionary*.

8. Rachel Brownstein, *Becoming A Heroine* (New York: Penguin Books, 1984) makes the point that the actual rape is incidental to Clarissa's story saying that the relationship to writing and the imagination is what is at stake in the novel. Clarissa exists only in letters, and Lovelace's rape is an effect of metaphor and imagination.

9. Madeleine Grumet, *Bitter Milk* (Amherst: University of Massachusetts Press, 1988).

10. Sigmund Freud, "Femininity," in *New Introductory Lectures to Psychoanalysis* (New York: Penguin Books, 1964) pp. 145–169.

11. Nel Noddings, *Caring* (Berkeley: University of California Press, 1984); Jane Roland Martin, *Reclaiming a Conversation* (New Haven: Yale University Press, 1985).

12. Elizabeth Young-Bruehl, "The Education of Women as Philosophers," *Signs,* 12:2, Winter 1987, pp. 222–254.

13. See, in particular, Jacques Derrida, *Of Grammatology* (Baltimore: Johns Hopkins University Press, 1976) and elsewhere, and Luce Irigaray, *Speculum of the Other Woman* (Ithaca: Cornell University press, 1985).

14. Virginia Woolf, *A Room of One's Own* (New York: Harcourt Brace Jovanovich, 1957), p. 68.

15. Rene Descartes, "Meditation One: Concerning Those Things That Can Be Called Into Doubt" in *Meditations on First Philosophy* (Indianapolis: Hackett Publishing Company, 1980).

16. Stanley Cavell, in *The Claim of Reason* (Cambridge: Oxford University Press, 1982) first identified for me the nature of the problem of relationship in Cartesian other-minds skepticism naming its association with trust and tragedy.

17. Bob Dylan, "Bob Dylan's Dream" from the album *Freewheelin'*, Columbia Records, 1961.

18. Ibid.

19. Lewis Carroll, *Through the Looking Glass* (Signet Classics, 1973).

20. Tony Tanner, *"Wuthering Heights* and *Jane Eyre"* in

Teaching the Text, Susanne Kappeler and Norman Bryson, eds. (Boston: Routledge and Kegan Paul, 1983).

21. Charlotte Brontë, *Jane Eyre* (New York: W. W. Norton & Company, 1971).

22. Adrienne Rich, "Jane Eyre: The Temptations of a Motherless Woman," *On Lies, Secrets, and Silences: Selected Prose, 1966–1973* (New York: W. W. Norton & Company, 1979).

23. Brontë, *Jane Eyre*, pp. 95–96.

24. Sandra M. Gilbert and Susan Gubar, "A Dialogue of Self and Soul: Plain Jane's Progress," *The Madwoman in the attic* (New Haven: Yale University Press, 1979).

25. Margaret Homans, *Bearing the Word*.

26. Jane Gallop, *The Daughter's Seduction: Feminism and Psychoanalysis* (Ithaca, New York: Cornell University Press, 1983), p. 45.

27. Virginia Woolf, *A Room of One's Own*, p. 103.

28. Madeleine Grumet, "Conception, Contradiction, and Curriculum," *Journal of Curriculum Theorizing* 3, no. 1 (Winter, 1981) pp. 289–298.

29. Ibid.

30. Ibid.

31. Madeleine Grumet, "My Face Is Thine Eye, Thine in Mine Appeares: The Look of Parenting and Pedagogy," *Phenomenology + Pedagogy*, 1:1, 1983.

32. Ibid., p. 55.

33. Ibid., p. 56.

34. See Gilbert and Gubar, *The Madwoman in the Attic*.

35. See Margaret Homans, *Bearing the Word*.

36. Woolf, *A Room of One's Own*, pp. 48–50.

37. Mary Wollstonecraft, *A Vindication of the Rights of Woman* (New York: W. W. Norton & Company, 1975).

38. Susan Stanford Friedman, "Authority in the Feminist

Classroom: A Contradiction in Terms?" in *Gendered Subjects* Catherine Portuges and Margo Culley, editors (London: Routledge Kegan Paul, 1985), pp. 203–208.

39. Gilbert Ryle, *The Concept of Mind* (New York: Harper & Row, 1949).

40. Israel Scheffler, *Reason and Teaching* (New York: Bobbs-Merrill, 1973).

41. Neil Hertz, "Two Extravagant Teachings," *Teaching as a Literary Genre*, Barbara Johnson, ed. (New Haven: Yale University Press, 1982).

42. See Ludwig Wittgenstein, *Philosophical Investigations* (New York: MacMillan, 1953) and Thomas Morawetz's analysis of *On Certainty* in *Wittgenstein and Knowledge* (Amherst: The University of Massachusetts Press, 1978).

43. Steven Unger, "The Professor of Desire," in *Teaching as a Literary Genre*, Barbara Johnson, editor (New Haven: Yale University Press, 1982) pp. 81–97.

44. Plato, "Phaedrus," in *The Collected Dialogues*, Edith Hamilton and Huntington Cairns, eds.(Princeton University Press, Bollinger Series, 1971).

45. R. S. Peters, *Ethics and Education* (London: George Allen & Unwin, 1966).

46. Stanley Fish, *Is There A Text In This Class?* (Cambridge: Harvard University Press, 1980).

47. Ibid., p. 360.

48. Ibid., p. 367.

49. Stephen Toulmin, *The Place of Reason in Ethics* (Cambridge: Oxford University Press, 1980).

50. Stanley Cavell, *The Claim of Reason: Wittgenstein, Skepticism, Morality, and Tragedy* (Oxford University Press, 1982).

51. Jacques Lacan, *Feminine Sexuality*, Juliet Mitchell and Jacqueline Rose, editors (New York: W. W. Norton, 1985).

52. Ludwig Wittgenstein, *Philosophical Investigations*.

53. Stanley Cavell, *The Claim of Reason*.

54. Susanne Kappeler and Norman Bryson, eds., *Teaching the Text* (London: Routledge & Kegan Paul, 1983).

55. Stanley Cavell, *The Claim of Reason*.

56. Stanley Cavell, Ibid.

57. Stanley Cavell, Ibid.

58. Margaret Homans, *Bearing the Word*.

59. I am indebted for this characterization of the houses in terms of gender politics to a lecture given by Professor Jill Harsin of the Colgate University History Department.

60. Stanley Cavell, *The Claim of Reason*, p. 25.

61. Madeleine Grumet, "Conception, Contradiction, and the Curriculum," *Journal of Curriculum Theorizing*, 3:1 (Winter, 1981) pp. 287.

62. Ralph Waldo Emerson, "The American Scholar," *Five Essays on Man and Nature*, Robert E. Spiller, ed. (Illinois: Harlan Davidson, Inc., 1954) p. 44.

63. Shoshana Felman, "Psychoanalysis and Education: Teaching Terminable and Interminable," in *The Pedagogical Imperative*, Barbara Johnson, editor (New Haven: Yale University Press, 1982), pp. 21–44.

64. Sandra M. Gilbert and Susan Gubar, *The Madwoman in the Attic* (New Haven: Yale University Press, 1982).

65. See the essays in *Gendered Subjects*, Margo Culley and Catherine Portuges, eds. (London: Routledge & Kegan Paul, 1985).

66. For a full account of women's peculiar relationship to the authority of language, see Jacques Lacan, *Feminine Sexuality*, Juliet Mitchell and Jacqueline Rose, eds. (New York: W. W. Norton, 1985); Jane Gallop's reading of the relationship between Lacan and Luce Irigaray in *The Daughter's Seduction* (Ithaca: Cornell University Press, 1982); Luce Irigaray, *This Sex Which Is Not One* (Ithaca: Cornell University Press, 1985), and *Speculum of the Other Woman*

(Ithaca: Cornell University Press, 1985). And of course see also Margaret Homans, *Bearing the Word*.

67. Nel Noddings, *Caring*.

68. Jane Roland Martin, *Reclaiming a Conversation;* "The Ideal of the Educated Person," *Educational Theory* 31:2 (Spring 1981); and "Bringing Women into Educational Thought," *Educational Theory* 34:4 (Fall 1984).

69. Madeleine Grumet, *Bitter Milk* (Amherst: University of Massachusetts Press, 1988).

70. Stanley Cavell, *The Claim of Reason*.

71. E. Anne Kaplan, *Women and Film* (New York: Methuen, 1983).

72. Sandra M. Gilbert and Susan Gubar, *The Madwoman in the Attic*.

73. Lillian Robinson, "Treason Our Text: Feminist Challenges to the Literary Canon," and Jane P. Tompkins, "Sentimental Power: *Uncle Tom's Cabin* and the Politics of Literary History," *Feminist Criticism: Essays on Women, Literature & Theory*, Elaine Showalter, ed. (New York: Pantheon Books, 1985).

74. Margaret Homans, *Bearing the Word*.

75. Madeleine R. Grumet, "Where The Line Is Drawn," in *Bitter Milk* (Amherst: University of Massachusetts Press, 1988), pp. 77–94.

76. Susan Gubar, "The Blank Page and the Issue of Female Creativity," in *Feminist Criticism*, p. 292.

77. Rachel M. Brownstein, *Becoming a Heroine* (New York: Penguin Books, 1984).

78. Claude Bernard, *An Introduction to the Study of Experimental Medicine* (New York: Dover, 1957).

79. May Sarton, *The Small Room* (New York: W. W. Norton, 1961), p. 29.

80. Ibid., p. 163.

81. Neil Hertz, "Two Extravagant Teachings," in *The*

Pedagogical Imperative, p. 60, quoting from "A Writer's Responsibilities," which was in turn excerpted from Harold C. Martin, *The Logic and Rhetoric of Exposition* (New York: Holt, 1958).

82. Ibid., pp. 61, 62.

83. Ibid., p. 63.

84. May Sarton, *The Small Room*, p. 200.

85. Ibid., p. 201.

86. Virginia Woolf, *A Room of One's Own*, pp. 90–94.

87. It should be understood that I am not making biological or universal claims in my use of psychological theory. With Simone de Beauvoir and others, I assume that gender is made within our relational experiences of same- and different-sexed others and that our ways of making gender emerge from a social, political, and economic complex, which is in turn influenced by our ways of making gender and by our relational experiences of gender.

88. Nancy Chodorow, *The Reproduction of Mothering: Psychoanalysis and the Sociology of Gender* (Berkeley: University of California Press, 1978).

89. Sigmund Freud, "Femininity," in *New Introductory Lectures on Psychoanalysis* (Hammondsworth, England: Penguin, 1933).

90. Sigmund Freud, *Dora: An Analysis of a Case of Hysteria* (New York: Macmillan, 1963.) See also the essays on this case collected in *In Dora's Case: Freud, Hysteria, Feminism*, Charles Bernheimer and Claire Kahane, eds. (London: Virago Press, 1985).

91. Elizabeth Abel, "Narrative Structure(s) and Female Development: The Case of *Mrs. Dalloway*," in *The Voyage In: Fictions of Female Development*, Elizabeth Abel, Marianne Hirsch, and Elizabeth Langland, eds. (Hanover, N.H.: University Press of New England, 1983), pp. 161–185.

92. Nadya Aisenberg and Mona Harrington, *Women of Academe* (Amherst: University of Massachusetts Press, 1988).

93. May Sarton, *The Small Room*, p. 102.

94. Ibid., p. 125, 126.

95. Ibid., p. 204.

96. Ibid., p. 234.

97. Ibid., p. 249.

98. Ibid., p. 237.

99. Virginia Woolf, *A Room of One's Own* (New York: Harcourt Brace Jovanovich, 1929). Much of the use I shall make of Woolf's essay I owe to a lecture given in a Colgate University course entitled "Interdisciplinary Perspectives on Women," by Professor Jane Pinchin.

100. Virginia Woolf, *A Room of One's Own*, p. 52.

101. Ibid., p. 6.

102. Gubar, "The Blank Page and Issues of Female Creativity."

103. Luce Irigaray, *This Sex Which Is Not One,* and *Speculum of the Other Woman.*

104. Elizabeth Young-Bruehl, "The Education of Women as Philosophers," *Signs* 12:2 (Winter 1987), pp. 207–21.

105. See, for example, Pierre Bourdieu, "The School as a Conservative Force: Scholastic and Cultural Inequalities," in *Value and Social Research,* Walter Feinberg and Eric Bredo, editors (Philadelphia: Temple University Press, 1980) pp. 391–407.

106. Maxine Hong Kingston, *The Woman Warrior* (New York: Vintage, 1977).

107. This was part of a much televised advertisement in 1985 for a product which I no longer remember.

108. Virginia Woolf, *Three Guineas* (New York: Harcourt Brace and Company, 1938) pp. 92, 93.

109. Virginia Woolf, "Professions for Women," in *Virginia Woolf: Women and Writing,* Michelle Barrett, ed. (New York: Harcourt Brace Jovanovich, 1979) pp. 59, 60.

110. Margaret Homans points out the significance of this conjunction of events in *Bearing the Word.* Homans argues it

reveals Woolf's own ambivalence to the maternal project. Her losing her grandmother's brooch is a sign of her disdain for her maternal heritage and her eagerness to align herself with the male order. At the same time, her leaving an unfinished *Middlemarch* on the train is a sign of Woolf's insistence that women kill the Angel, and quit telling the kinds of stories women tell.

111. Virginia Woolf, *A Room of One's Own*.

112. Sigmund Freud, *Dora*, p. 65.

113. Jane Gallop, *The Daughter's Seduction*, p. 141.

114. Jane Roland Martin, *Reclaiming a Conversation*.

115. Jonathan Culler, *On Deconstruction*.

116. Ibid.

117. Jane Roland Martin, *Reclaiming a Conversation*.

118. Jean Elshtain, "Feminist Discourse and Its Discontents: Language, Power, and Meaning," in *Feminist Theory: A Critique of Ideology*, Nanerl O. Keohane, Michelle Z. Rosaldo, and Barbara C. Gelpi, eds. (Chicago: The University of Chicago Press, 1982) pp. 127–146.